# Making Floral Designs

# Making Floral Designs

## Pamela Woods

line drawings by Vanessa Woods

B T Batsford Ltd, London

# Acknowledgements

I should like to thank Vanessa Woods for the line illustrations and Roland Prosser for supplying the photographs. My special thanks also to Diane Hannant for typing all my work and for her unending support. There are few people who give their time so generously and I shall always be grateful to her.

ISBN 0 7134 4225 5 (cased)

Typeset by Tek-Art Ltd Kent
and printed in Great Britain by
R J Acford
Chichester, Sussex
for the publishers
B.T. Batsford Ltd
4 Fitzhardinge Street
London W1H 0AH

# Contents

# Introduction

The creative art of flowermaking develops from the love of flowers. Many people say to me 'Why do you have so many artificial flowers, don't you prefer real ones?' The answer to this is simple, it is the love and fascination of real flowers which inspires the creative mind and so leads to investigation and a deeper knowledge. To recreate flowers, observation not only of plant structure, but colour, climate and peculiar characteristics is important. But exact replicas are not the sole aim, it is the essence and character of a flower type which should be captured. And for this the appropriate material should be used. Thin and light materials, for example, will be suitable for the daisy or composite family, as the petals are thin and plentiful. Most petals curl as they open so the material should also be able to be shaped by hand or held in shape with wire supports. Not many flowers are patterned all over, but shading is often an essential element and this should be noticed and, where applicable, imitated. The position of the stamens is another point to look for and imitate, just as is the angle of the flower head. Notice also how the floral stem grows – straight, curved or twisted – and how it grows from the main stem, bulb or root. It is important to extract only the essential elements as over-worked petals or leaves often destroy the quality of the material, which should contribute to the overall design.

Flowers fall into definite types according to their botanical families, such as roses, lilies, bells, daisies, tulips, to name but a few.

The instructions which follow are based on observations of types of flower and the materials have been chosen to suit not only the flower but also the design in which it plays a part. They are not intended to be followed slavishly but used as a guide or inspiration for your own creative ability.

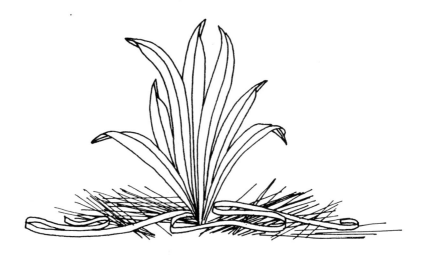

# 1 Materials and Manipulation

For those who love flowers it is always a little sad when fresh flowers give up their life and disappear. The way to extend or capture some of the qualities we appreciate in flowers is to make them. To create exact replicas, however, is usually beyond the possibilities of the floral artist but, by the choice of an interesting material, the artist can add another dimension. Real flowers are delicate objects which do not withstand overhandling and this is equally true of manufactured ones.

## SHAPING

Whichever material is chosen, it is worth investing a little time in considering how it should be used. Most materials can be glued and wired and with the exception of paper, stitched. Pleating and plaiting (figs 1a and 1b) can be applied, with care, to both paper and fabric. Ribbons fall into both categories, as the stiffened, water-repellent ones are like paper and the woven-edged are narrow fabrics. Feathers have to be assessed individually for their flexibility. Most are too brittle or fragile but do not be afraid to reshape them, if necessary, by cutting. All materials can be threaded (fig. 1c) providing it is possible either to make a hole or to insert the threading material. When curls are required these are, where possible, made by drawing the material over the blade of a knife (fig. 1e). In the case of feathers, this action is likely to detroy the whole structure, so care has to be taken to squeeze the vein into a curve over a blade rather than to pull it. Crepe paper has crinkles which can be stretched into different shapes. For example, when stretched in the centre a dome or cup emerges or when stretched at the edge the paper becomes frilled.

Where a material cannot support itself, in spite of moulding, coiling or pleating, it has to have the addition of a wire support. The wire should either be paper covered or cotton covered, as in milliners' wire, and, whether placed through the centre or round the edge of the material, it should tone with the petals or leaves. Remember that any glue applied

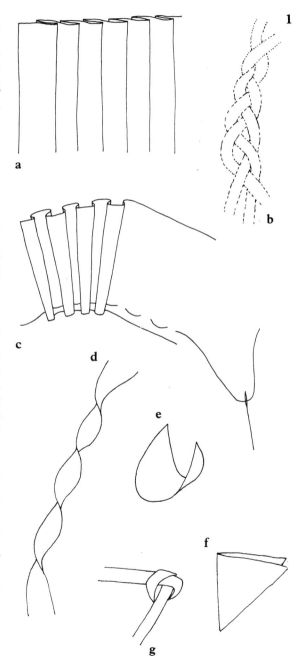

to the wire should be kept to the smallest area. Also, ensure that the wire reaches the very tip of the leaf or petal shape so that the curve is created from tip to stem; any overlapping material will inevitably flop. The curl or uplift at the tip enhances the whole shape of the flower or leaf.

## FLOWER ASSEMBLY

There are only three basic ways in which a flower can be assembled, according to the way in which the petals are attached. Naturally, there are many permutations, but the basic three are: a disc of petals into which the centre of the flower is inserted; a strip of petals which are wrapped arouund the stem; individual petals applied separately. When assembling flowers always bear in mind the function of the petals which is to first protect the seed and then handsomely display it for propagation. Hence they should be attached at the same level around the seed. Be careful not to work lower and lower down the stem. This can often happen when, for example, you are assembling roses with many petals and it could result in an unsightly spiral of descending petals.

During the process of making the flowers there are several points which should be borne in mind and which are essential for successful flowermaking. Before starting any flower to which the material is bound to a stem, use a reel of binding wire and a stem wire, and, starting 2.5 cm (1 in.) from the top, wind the thinner wire in a spiral to the top (fig. 2a). To make it secure bend this bound part over to form a loop and wind the wire round the two once or twice (fig. 2b). Never cut off the binding wire until the complete flower is finished and always bind as tightly as possible to prevent any pieces coming away and falling off.

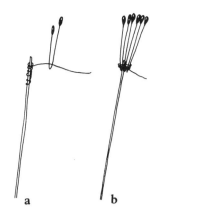

Choose, if posible, the lightest workable binding wire as this is the easiest to manipulate, but it should not break every time it is pulled. It is most likely that a heavier binding wire is more successful with heavier materials. Then choose the relative stem wire to go with it. This should be about 10 sizes stronger. If the stem does not support the finished flower head, it is a simple process to add extra wire when binding the stem and then to tape over the original and the new wire.

## STAMENS

When stamens are needed, they can be bound to the stem first before any petals are attached. Join the binding wire to the stem wire as previously instructed but do not make the hook on the top. As many stamens come with a head on each end, they should be folded to make all the heads face the same way. It is always interesting to vary the height of the stamen heads so do not fold them too accurately in half (fig. 3a). Then insert the binding wire inside the fold of the stamens and, holding them closely together, make one or two tight binds with the binding wire (fig. 3b). Unlike petals, several stamens can be added at the same time. Some flowers, such as poppies, have stamens as well as a large central seed pod. This can take the shape of a little sack, bead or cotton mould which is glued or bound to the top of the stem first. Then the stamens are added in sections until the perimeter of the seed pod is filled. For lilies and fuchsias the stamens protrude and play a prominent part in the profile of the flower. So the length of the adjoining petals should allow the stamens to be visible. It may be necessary to attach the petals at a lower point on the stem. There are times, however, when this is not possible without the wire showing, so in these cases it is advisable to cover the wire with matching tape before assembling the petals.

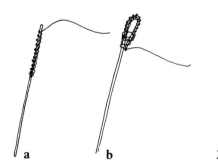

## STEM BINDING

Finished flowers are covered with floral tape to conceal all the unsightly bases to the petals and wire. Start this binding by attaching the adhesive tape, squeezing the stem and rotating it. Start on the wire just below the base of the petals so that the tape is anchored before working up over the unsightly material. Continue rotating until the mechanics are completely covered, and then allow the tape to work down the stem. Always make sure that the tape is flat and taut; many kinds of tape are in fact self-adhesive crepe paper and the crinkles should be stretched flat as the stem is bound. The stem covering must not move once it is in position on the wire. Check by squeezing the stem together and pulling the tape down the stem. If it protrudes below the wire then the binding is not tight enough. A tightly bound stem is necessary not only because a loose and uneven one is unsightly but also because the covering and not the wire holds the flower in its position. When sprays of leaves or flowers are to be assembled, each component should be completed separately, including the stem binding. One long main stem should, however, bear one of the flowers or leaves so that the other components of the design can simply be held in position beside this main stem and then taped together. A tightly bound stem is essential, otherwise the components will swing around. Any shaping of the stem, as for instance for pendulous flowers, is made by bending the stem once the flower is completed.

## WIRING

Many leaves and grasses have to be broken from the main stem to be used individually, so require an artificial stem. To do this, place a stem wire beside the material stem so that both are the same length. Then bend the wire over to form a small hook and wind the longest length of wire tightly round the two shorter stems. Cover this with tape.

## COWEE PICKS

When the techniques of wiring have been mastered, you will find cowee picks can cut assembly time in half, as they already have a thin binding wire attached. All you have to do is to hold a stem alongside a stick and, holding the end of the wire away, spin the two and the wire will automatically bind them (fig. 4). So many times you can find

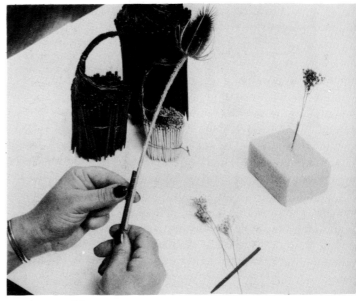

4   *Cowee picks*

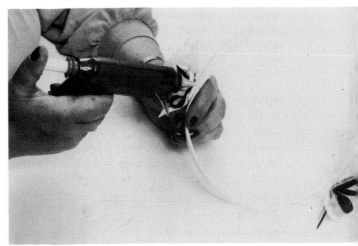

5   *Glue gun*

6   *Flower former*

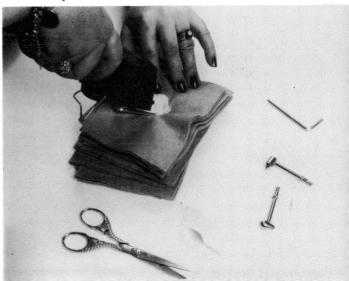

yourself in the situation where a fragile or soft stem will not penetrate the foam, a bunch of small material requires a major stem, or a leaf needs an extension stem, cowee picks solve the problem quickly and efficiently. Available in various lengths and widths, they can be used as extensions by adding one to another and flowers with only a few petals can be assembled straight onto them.

## TOOLS

There are two tools which a floral designer will not work without. One is a glue gun (fig. 5) which is quick and efficient, making it possible to stick together all materials, from the tiniest piece of grass to the heaviest fir cone. The other is an electric flower former (fig. 6), a modern version of the flower iron. This tool comes with various attachments and can be heated as hot as an iron. Pressed into fabrics it will create indentations. Whether you want veins for leaves, curls on petals, or crinkled edges, the flower former will produce the shape. It is important to test the fabric concerned with the former first, however, to ensure the heat is not so high as to cause damage.

## COLOURING

Sometimes a change of colour is required; most materials can be dyed, coloured or painted. Spray paints are ideal for gentle colouring as they coat the material thinly and dry very quickly. There are spray paints which can be purchased especially for flowers. Offered in realistic floral colours, they can give various effects, ranging from gentle partial tints to a total change of colour, according to the amount used. These sprays are ideal when a colour emphasis is required in the centre of a flower, as no hard edge results. Wax, when melted, can be used as a coating material; it can be used for decorating or even for moulding into three-dimensional forms. To use wax, all that is required are the odd remains of old candles melted down. Once the wicks are removed simply dip the flowerhead so that it is submerged completely and remove very quickly spinning the stem in the process so that no globules of wax are allowed to set on the petals. There are, however, two points to bear in mind when working with hot wax; firstly, it is absolutely essential not to let it reach smoking point as wax is highly inflammable, so be sure to work over a very low heat; and secondly, when spinning the flower, watch that the splashes

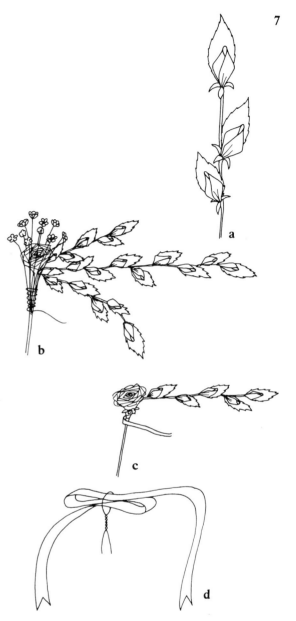

are contained within the area of the saucepan, as it is quite surprising how far wax will fly if the flower is spun up in the air. It is a good idea to have a large empty box nearby in which to do the spinning. Wax can be an interesting dip for some rather plain materials such as paper, felt and fleece, as it gives a translucent quality to the material which breaks down its denseness. Another quality is the waterproofing it can give an absorbent material, thus enabling it to be used with fresh foliage or even floating in water. Both wax and dye can be combined for batik decoration.

Some materials such as silks, lace and flimsy papers are inviting by virtue of their colour and delicacy, but they do not have the substance to support themselves. They can be given wire supports, or strengthened by starching. There are various commercial spray starches available, but an ordinary jelly dissolved in an equal amount of water can be used just as effectively. The colour of the jelly will be transferred to the fabric and thus some delicate shades can be created on white or very pale fabrics. On darker materials the colour of the jelly will have no effect.

## CHOOSING THE DESIGN

Whether you wish to make a conventional flower arrangement of flowers in a vase or a less conventional one such as a picture on the wall, the balance and colour of the design are the most important considerations. By balance is meant aspects of size, weight, outline and the relationship of one flower to another. Another important consideration is where the arrangement is intended to be placed. Is it to be worn or is it to be placed in a setting? For example, in a room setting, the background against which the flowers will be seen plays an important part in your choice of colour, balance and proportion. Some people prefer their flowers to blend with the background, whereas others like to see flowers contrasting. Some people prefer their floral designs to be tonal shades around one colour, others will combine several colours successfully. An assortment of colours can be beautiful when chosen well but too many different materials, on the other hand, can deter from the final effect.

It is preferable to use several colours of the same material with perhaps one or two additions, than to have a conglomeration of mixed materials and colours. Often a particular material demands a contrast; for example, felt can appear somewhat heavy, so dried grasses would enhance and soften the effect.

When you have selected colours, materials, position and size of design, there is still the type of flower to be decided upon. Whether the design is to have many flowers or only a few, a variation in size of flower will enhance the effect. Imagine a line of flowers of identical size, then imagine a line of flowers decreasing in size. The second is visually more acceptable because the line gives an illusion of perspective. Choose large flowers at the focal point, then some smaller ones and foliage. Decide how you

wish each flower to be viewed, from the front or the side. One effective arrangement is: full face focal flowers with the smaller flowers in profile as so many flowers have a round outline when viewed from the front, but provide an interesting variation in shape from the side. These suggestions are merely intended as guidelines.

The method of arranging also varies according to whether the flowers are to be in a container or not. For a traditional floral arrangement in a vase, stem holders such as floral foam, pinholders, straw, moss or marbles can be used to support the stems. There are various types of floral foam, for instance. The green 'wet' foam is made to absorb water and, therefore, to be used with fresh flowers. The brown 'dry' foam is for all dry and artificial stems, and it comes in different shapes. If you decide to use a basket as a container, bear in mind there are two types: those which will take a liner and traditional stem supports, and those which are too flat for this and have to have the spray of flowers assembled first and then attached. The spray can either be wired through the basket, tied on with ribbon or glued with a glue gun. This last method is the most permanent but if you wish to change the flowers, one of the other two methods might be better. For attaching flowers to panels or other solid backing, the glue gun is undoubtedly the best. If a glue gun is not available, tubular glues are possible but they take so much longer to set and you have to hold or support the position of the flower until the glue holds it. The glue from the gun holds as it cools which is almost instantly.

To assemble a spray, or bouquet, work in exactly the same way as the spray of leaves or flowers, that is by taping the stems together. For example, if a traditional bouquet shape is required, first make a long trail of flowers and leaves. Start with the smallest material at the end of the main supporting stem and, placing the leaves behind the flowers as if to support them, work down the stem, increasing the size of the material in the process. Try to place the flowers at irregular intervals and avoid allowing them to lie in a straight line. Make sure that the flowers face the general flow of the stem so that most of them are seen from the side. When the spray achieves the required length, take one large focal flower and tape this to arrest the flow. At this point, bend the stem so that this flower is on a straight stem which will form the handle and as the trail flows out to one side. If more trails are required, make each one separately and fix it below the focal flower to what will now be termed the fixing point. At this stage exchange the tape binding material for

**8a, b, c and d** *Spray in four ways*

binding wire as it is stronger and less bulky. Do not undo any of the tape binding, just break it off and continue with wire. Now work around the focal flower, first by adding medium-sized flowers, binding each one on individually. This part of the bouquet is assembled in the same way as petals are bound together to make a flower. Place the flowers in an irregular halo around the focal flower, grouping areas of colour if the flowers are small. When the required size is reached and this central part appears to be a beautiful cluster of flowers to cover the hand, extend the edge with small buds and leaves. The whole spray should have a delicate outline, so it is advisable to check that no larger flower is at the perimeter which will give an abrupt edge. When placing the flowers in the central area be sure to recess one or two full blooms as short as possible so that none of the binding is showing. Two sides are twice as visible as the one facing the front so the shape and design of the flowers here are just as, if not more important than the front. Arrange them so that some longer stems create a gentle dome; try to avoid a flat appearance.

A contrast in texture is sometimes welcome and this can be achieved with fluffy marabou feathers or delicate sprays of gypsophila. In the case of the marabou, the fluffy material should be intermingled with the flowers themselves, but the gypsophila should be longer as if to create a hazy halo.

When the flowers are all in position, cover the collection of stems with tape. A trail of ribbon to display the trail of flowers is added next. Measure the length required and cut the ribbon three times as long. Double-sided satin ribbon is the most suitable for this. Fold the ribbon in half across the centre and while holding at this point, make a loop with the ribbon on each side. One or several loops can be made at this point by making the ribbon zig-zag so that the loops fall on alternate sides. Then take a covered stem wire, place it over the ribbon at the point where it is held and twist the ends together as tightly as possible to form a stem. As the wire tightens around the ribbon, the loops will stand up. It is always possible to ease the loops apart if they overlap. These wires will be hard to hold, particularly if satin ribbon is to be used to cover the handle, so take a strip of paper handkerchief and bind the handle with it first. To cover with ribbon, first cut a piece three times the length of the handle and find the point one third along its length. Attach this to the base of the handle with glue. Then, holding the short piece beside the handle, wrap it with the longer length as tightly as possible. When the handle is bound right to the flowers tie the two ends together with a tight knot. Make a beautiful bow behind the flowers and allow the trails to cascade behind the flowers. Trim the ends of the ribbon diagonally, cutting one shorter than the other. The ribbons should be slightly longer than the flowers to extend the line of the bouquet.

Having mastered the technique of making the bouquet this can be adapted to any shape of spray, whether it is carried, displayed on the wall or attached to a basket (figs 8a, b, c and d).

# **2** The Flowers

In this chapter you will find all the instructions for making the flowers which follow in the designs later on. The instructions are also intended to be used as inspiration and guidelines for your own creations. Any materials are worth experimenting with and the designs can be adapted to whatever materials you choose. Since it is the style of the flower which is important, the actual size can vary according to the design into which it is to be placed. To give variety within your arrangements it is always advisable to make flowers of varying sizes. In the multi-petal flowers such as roses and daisies, however, a flower can be overcrowded with petals if it is too small, or can appear somewhat empty if it is too large. In such cases the size and quantities of elements must be thought about carefully.

Any support needed can be given by means of additional wires or those of a heavier gauge, depending on the weight of the material.

**POPPY FIELD**

It is rather fun sometimes to put man-made flowers in a natural setting. Shirley poppies (*see page 39*) in tissue paper, are used here, in the field.

# WIRED LEAF CAMELIA

# WIRED LEAF LILY

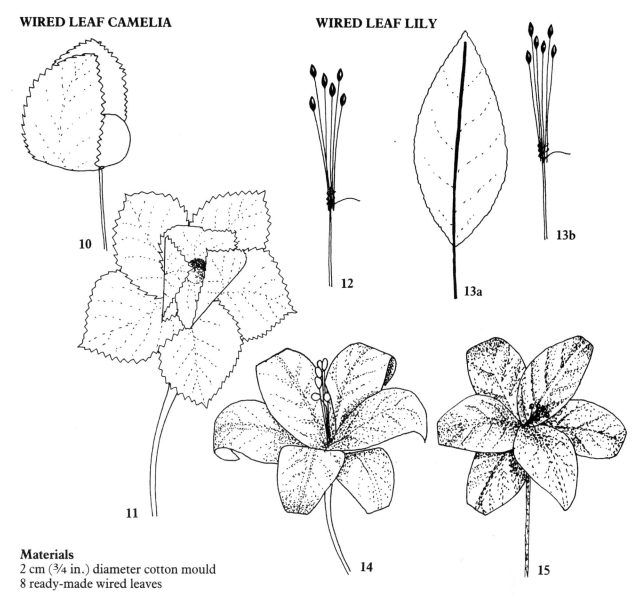

10

11

12

13a

13b

14

15

## Materials
2 cm (¾ in.) diameter cotton mould
8 ready-made wired leaves

First cover the stem with tape and then insert it with glue into the cotton mould. Trim away the serrated edges from the base of the leaves and bind three of these so that they face inwards around the cotton mould. Curve the tips inwards so that they completely cover the cotton mould in the centre. Then add each of the five remaining leaves separately and curl these outwards so that they radiate evenly from the centre petals. Cover all the wires beneath the petals with tape.

A variation can be made when the leaves are cut; you may prefer to have rounded petals, rather than pointed ones, or heart-shaped petals. This could be a matter for experiment.

## Materials
3 pairs white pearl stamens
6 ready-made wired leaves

Fold three pairs of stamens in half and bind them tightly to the top of the stem (fig. 12). Then cut away the serrated edges from the base of the leaves and bind three of them first to the stamens so that they are evenly spaced and then place the remaining three in the spaces between the first ones. Bind all the wires together with tape and then, starting at the tip of the petals, curl them outwards. When all the petals are curled, bend the stem so that the lily faces sideways.

15

# WIRED LEAF TULIP

# WIRED LEAF IRIS

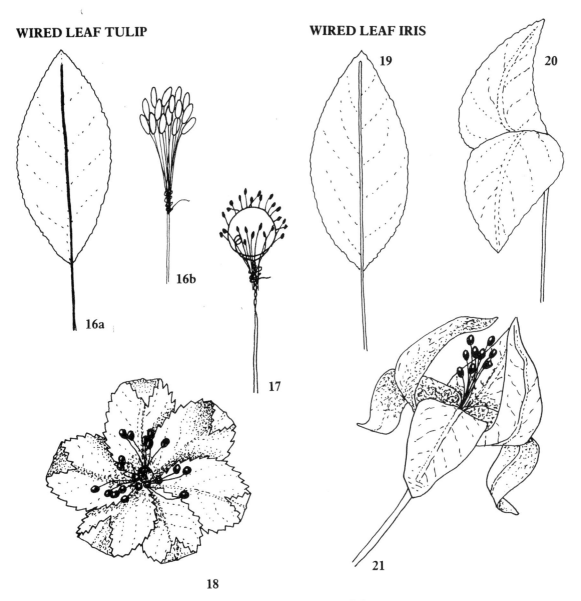

16a

16b

17

18

19

20

21

## Materials
1 assembled stamen centre
6 ready-made wired leaves

Stamens can be bought already assembled so, if possible, use them here. If not, purchase the separate components and assemble them yourself. Cut the serrated edges from each of the six wired leaves and wire each one individually around the stamen, adding at the same time a supporting stem wire. Tape all the wires and shape the petals by opening them out at the base under the stamens lifting them straight up the side and then curve the tip of the petals very slightly outwards.

## Materials
6 ready-made wired leaves (preferably two shades – three of each)

This flower is extremely simple to make as the wiring is already in place. Take three leaves of one shade and bind each one individually to a stem so that they encircle the stem once. Attach the second colour of leaves similarly. Trim away the serrated edges and curve the inside first layer of petals outwards and downwards so that they overlap the outside layer. Then open the last outside layer out first and then curve the tips in so that they join over the top of the centre. You may prefer to make the falls rounded, simply cut the shape you require.

This little garden is made of styrofoam which is sprayed with glue and then covered with pot-pourri into which the little crocuses are planted at random to simulate the way in which they grow naturally. This design should really be viewed from the side and should be placed high up so that it is possible to look through the stems.

**Materials**

1 chenille stem
2 sheets yellow wood fibre
Green flock paper

First cut the chenille to a length of 5 cm (2 in.) and bind this to the top of a stem allowing half of it to extend beyond the stem (fig. 23). Cut six petals according to the pattern (fig. 24) and bind each one individually round the centre so that they overlap each other and radiate evenly from the chenille. For the leaves cut a strip with four points at irregular heights (fig. 25) and bind this strip around the base of the stem of the crocus. These little flowers are very effective made of tissue paper.

## WOOD FIBRE DAFFODIL

### Materials

7 x 2 cm (¾ in.) diameter cotton moulds
2 sheets shaded yellow/orange wood fibre
9 sheets plain yellow wood fibre
7 oval wooden beads
Tape for leaves

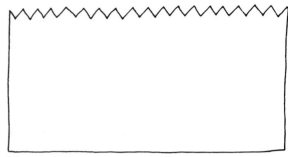

The quantities of materials above are for a complete plant of seven flowers, but the instructions which follow are only for one flower and then, of course, you must repeat for several flowers.

Cover the wire with tape and then attach the cotton mould to the top with glue. Cut the shaded sheet of wood fibre into four pieces and take one quarter and cut this to the dimensions 7.5 x 2.5 cm (3 x 1 in.), making a zig-zag top with pinking shears (fig. 27). Then, take one sheet of plain wood fibre. Fold this into half and half again and then cut all four layers together into the petal shape according to the pattern (fig. 28). Take a second sheet of this same plain wood fibre and repeat the process and use one of the petals from these so that you have five petals altogether for one daffodil. Take the strip first and apply glue to the widest part of the circumference of the cotton mould and wrap the wood fibre piece around it. This will form the trumpet of the daffodil. Then take one petal and attach it with glue to the lower part of the cotton mould and then continue in this way by adding each petal, overlapping the previous one very slightly until all five petals encircle the trumpet. Thread the oval bead on to the stem until it lies snugly behind the flower head. Tape right over the bead and the rest of the stem. Bend the flower head so that it faces sideways.

For the leaf, first cover the stem wire with tape and then apply a thin line of glue along this stem. Place it on to a flat strip of tape, fold the strip over the wire so that it is double with the wire sandwiched between the two layers (fig. 29). Cut the tip of leaf pointed and twist it slightly so that the whole leaf spirals.

For a complete plant you will need seven flowers and approximately fifteen leaves. Vary the length of the leaves so that they can fill the area between the flowers at irregular heights. This daffodil can also be made with paper as there is no moulding required and the stiff outline is then easily visible.

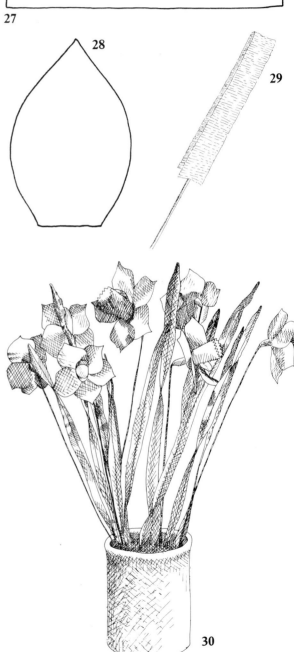

# AFRICAN VIOLETS

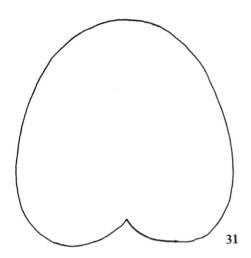

31

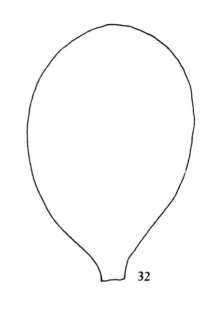

32

**Materials**
Ready-made forget-me-nots (*see page 28*)
Wood fibre
Artificial grass paper

The instructions that follow are for one flower which can be multiplied to form the whole African violet plant.

Separate the forget-me-nots so that each flower stands on its own stem. Bind to the top with binding wire, allowing the floral stem to stand 1.25 cm (½ in.) above the top of the stub wire. Fold one sheet of wood fibre in half and half again and then cut the four layers together into the petal shape according to the pattern (fig. 31). Bind one petal to the forget-me-not and then continue by adding each petal separately, overlapping each one very slightly in the process. Cover the binding and stem with tape. Then, using artificial grass paper, cut the leaf shape (fig. 32). First, cover the stem with tape and apply a thin line of glue and stick this to the back of the leaf. For a single plant, it is advisable to make double the number of leaves to the number of flowers and then arrange them so that the leaves form a small circle overlapping the sides of your container and then nestle the flowers between the leaves and in the centre. This little flower would also be effective made with tissue paper.

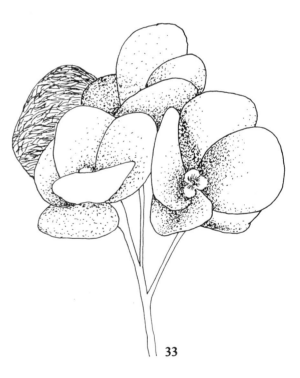

33

## WOOD FIBRE ROSE

### Materials
1 2.5 cm (1 in.) diameter cotton ball mould
4 sheets of shaded wood fibre

Cover the stem with tape and insert it into the cotton ball mould with glue (fig. 34a). Fold all the wood fibre in half and in half again and cut the layers together according to the pattern (fig. 34b). Take each petal separately and curl one side of each petal. Cut away a portion of the bases of the first five petals. Taking one petal only, apply glue round the circumference of the ball. Wrap this first petal around and close it over the ball so that it forms a point and continue to add the rest of these cut petals so that they encircle the original one. Then continue with the other petals adding each one separately so that it overlaps the previous one by half and gradually work the glue point further down the ball until the entire ball is covered. Finally, cover the stem again with tape. The flower is particularly beautiful when made with yellow wood fibre which is tinged with pink at the edge, closely resembling the 'Peace' rose.

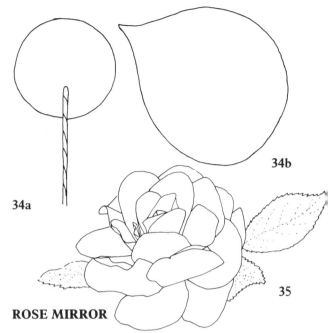

34b

34a

35

### ROSE MIRROR

This round mirror is a perfect setting for three wood fibre roses.

36

# FORSYTHIA

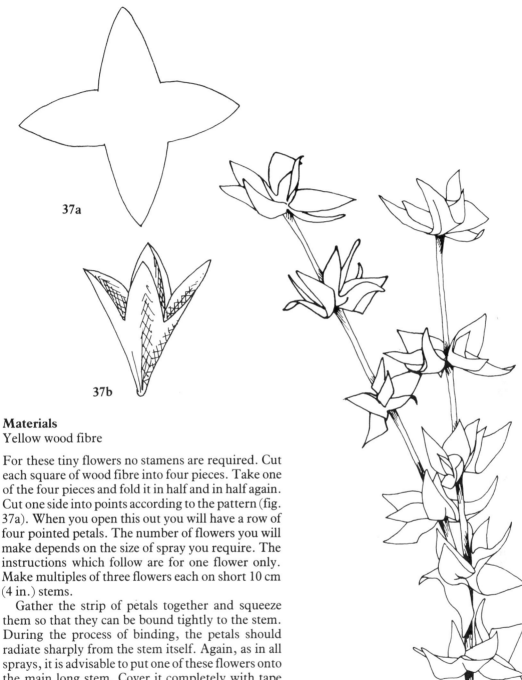

37a

37b

38

## Materials
Yellow wood fibre

For these tiny flowers no stamens are required. Cut each square of wood fibre into four pieces. Take one of the four pieces and fold it in half and in half again. Cut one side into points according to the pattern (fig. 37a). When you open this out you will have a row of four pointed petals. The number of flowers you will make depends on the size of spray you require. The instructions which follow are for one flower only. Make multiples of three flowers each on short 10 cm (4 in.) stems.

Gather the strip of petals together and squeeze them so that they can be bound tightly to the stem. During the process of binding, the petals should radiate sharply from the stem itself. Again, as in all sprays, it is advisable to put one of these flowers onto the main long stem. Cover it completely with tape and add the other flowers at intervals with more tape. The stem of forsythia normally consists of branches of sprays as well, so make up three or more sprays and again attach these to the original one. Ribbon and paper are also ideal for this particular flower.

# WOOD FIBRE CARNATION

# CATKINS

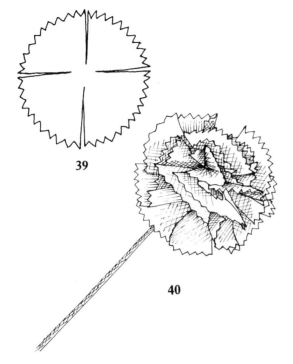

39

40

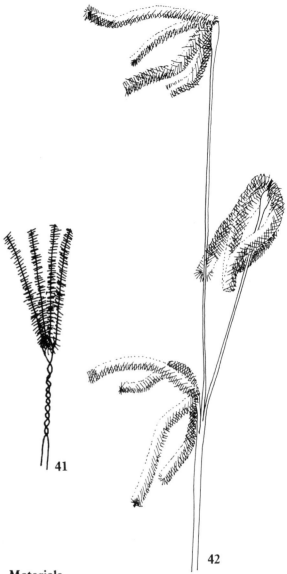

41

42

## Materials

1 oval bead 1.25 cm (½ in.) long
4 sheets red wood fibre paper
Pale cream tape

Take the four sheets together and fold them in half and in half again. Cut three quarters of the way along the folds leaving the centre of the sheet intact. Trim the edge with pinking shearts. When the sheets are flat they should appear according to the pattern (fig 39). Thread the oval bead on to a stem and fix it in position with a little glue at the top of the stem. Press the stem through the centre of one of the layers of wood fibre. Pull it right up over the bead and pinch it together securing this with glue. Continue adding each layer of wood fibre petals by threading each one in the same way. As each layer is glued into position the petals should be pulled up slightly so that they gather and undulate around each other. Finally, cover the stem with tape.

This flower can equally as well be made with tissue paper, although more layers would be needed as the material is so fine and loses its colour density. Taffeta and organdie are also suitable, but with the latter the edges tend to disappear, so it is advisable to brush over the top of the flower with paint, or as the Victorians used, lipstick. This will clarify the edges of the petals.

## Materials

Yellow chenille stems

Cut the chenille into 10 cm (4 in.) lengths and fold each one in half. The number you actually use depends on the length of stem you require for your arrangement. Repeat this process with all the remaining pieces of chenille. Join these catkin stems to a long supporting stem wire. Make one long spray with two supporting ones for branches, each spray to have three pairs of catkins. This should only act as guidance; you can, of course, vary these quantities. Arrange these stems so that all the catkins hang vertically downwards.

## PUSSY WILLOW

43

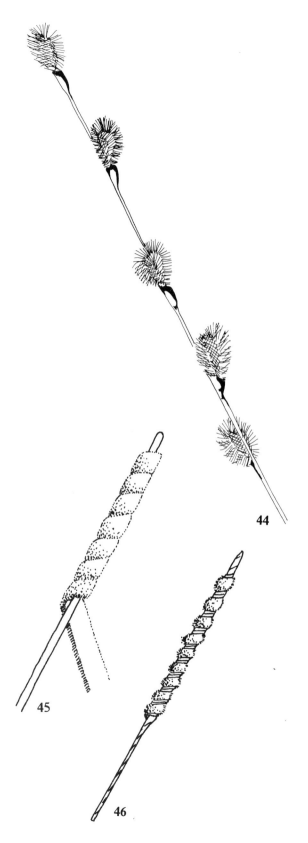

### Materials
Bump chenille

As pussy willow is a stem of little fluffy seed heads, cut the bump chenille so that each bump is separate (fig 43). The number of seeds you require on each stem is dependent on the length of stem needed for your arrangement. Take one of these bumps and fold it in half so that the wide part of the bump covers the loop of a long stem wire. Hold the narrow ends together and tape them to the wire. Work your tape only 10 cm (4 in.) down the stem and then add a second bump and continue by this process until all the bumps are attached. Arrange the bumps so that they lie in different positions on the stem.

44

## BULRUSHES

### Materials
Velvet ribbon 7 mm (¼ in.) wide

Apply a careful line of glue 10 cm (4 in.) long at the top of the stem wire. Hold the end of the velvet ribbon into position at the top of the wire. Rotate the wire with one hand while tightly spiralling the ribbon round as the wire turns (fig. 45). When the bulrush reaches the required length, trim away the end of the ribbon. Cover the end of the ribbon and stem with tape. This little bulrush is really more suitable for a small arrangement as the velvet is not thick enough to be very conspicuous in a large one.

45

46

# CHENILLE BULRUSHES

# CHENILLE STAR

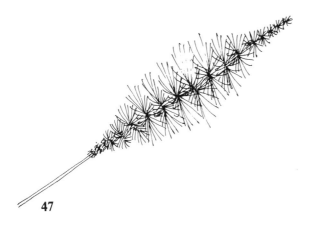

47

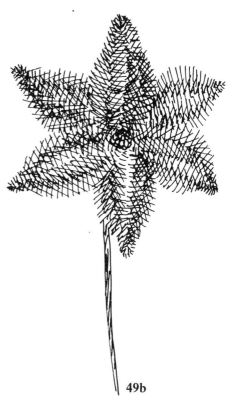

49b

**Materials**
Bump chenille

This is the most simple of bulrushes to make. Simply take one bump and twist it round the top of a stem. It is surprising how effective this shape is amongst many of the rounded floral shapes.

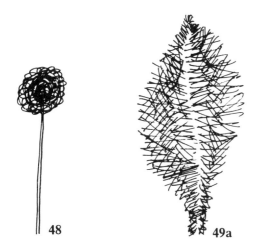

48

49a

**Materials**
2.5 cm (1 in.) gold bouillon
Length of 10 bumps of chenille

Stretch the bouillon very slightly and bind this over and over the top of a stem wire to form a little knot (fig. 48). Cut the chenille into five pairs of bumps. Fold each pair in half at the thinnest point squeezing it into a point and holding the two free ends together. Bind this to the centre. Continue with the other four pairs similarly until an evenly spaced star is created. The woolly texture of this flower can be a welcome contrast to some of the more solid flowers in an arrangement.

# CHENILLE FLOWER

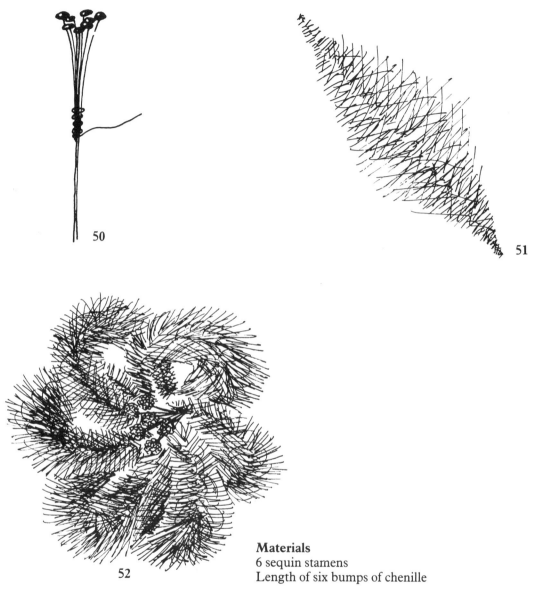

50

51

52

**Materials**
6 sequin stamens
Length of six bumps of chenille

Cut each of the bumps at the thinnest point to separate each one. Bind the six stamens to the top of a stem wire and loop each of the bumps over to form the shape of the petals. Taking one end of each bump, bind this to the stem so that all six pieces are surrounding the stamens. Continue binding and attach the other end of each petal so that it overlaps the next one. When all are completed this creates an interesting pattern. For an extra touch at Christmas spray with glitter; it does not spoil the fluffy look of the flower, but makes it sparkle.

# RIBBON PALM LEAF

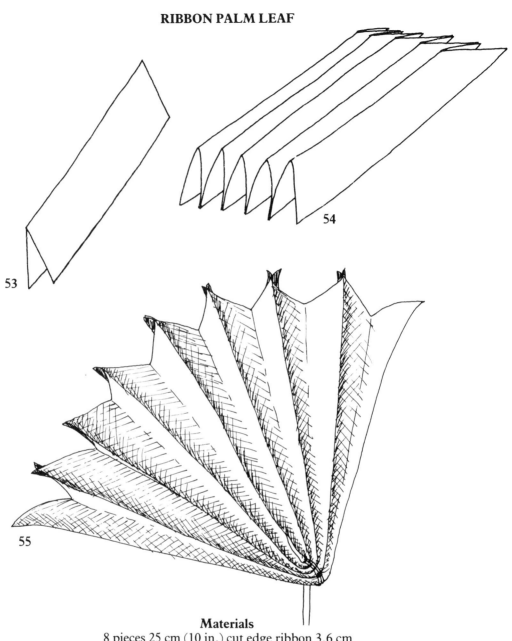

**Materials**
8 pieces 25 cm (10 in.) cut edge ribbon 3.6 cm
(1½ in.)

It is essential to use cut edge ribbon for this leaf as the water-repellent impregnated stiffness retains the shape of the palm. Cut 8 pieces 25 cm (10 in.) long and fold every piece in half lengthways (fig. 53). Apply a line of glue to the outside open edge of one of the pieces and attach a second one beside it. Continue by this process until all the pieces are joined together with the folds all on the same side and the open sides of the ribbon on the other (fig. 54). Before allowing this to spring open, cut one side diagonally to form points and wire the other side together very tightly with stem wire. Cover this with tape. The palm will spring open and the folds will retain the shape of the fan. It is essential for this leaf that a stiff material be used. However, paper is a very good substitute. Especially effective for Christmas is metallic, paperbacked foil.

26

56

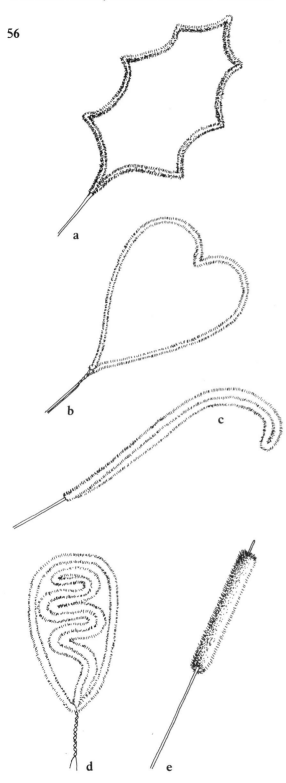

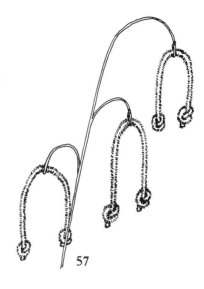

57

## Materials
Velvet tubing

Leaf
Wire can be inserted into velvet tubing and then twisted into many shapes. The simplest of all is the leaf. Insert a 30 cm (1 ft) stub wire into the tubing, cutting it so that a little piece of wire shows at each end. Join these ends together and bind and tape to a stem. The loop now formed can be shaped into a pointed leaf, a heart shape leaf, a zig-zag leaf or any other variation (fig. 56a-c). It can even be squeezed together completely flat and twisted like a daffodil leaf. To make a solid flat leaf, make one simple loop, then make another one, squeeze completely flat and zig-zag this inside the loop so that it fills the centre completely (fig. 56d).

Bulrush
Cut a piece of tubing 10 cm (4 in.) long. Insert a stem wire so that it extends beyond the top of the tubing. Bind this little piece of stem and the edge of the tubing with tape, then bind the lower part of the tubing and the rest of the stem also. These bulrushes can be made and stored for years. Should the tubing become crushed or tired looking, steam will revive it in a few minutes (fig. 56e).

Tubing willow
Cut a piece of velvet tubing 15 cm (6 in.) and knot each end. This tubing has no wire inside. Fold it in half and bind it to a stem at the fold, allowing the tubing to fall freely from an arched stem (fig. 57).

# FORGET-ME-NOT

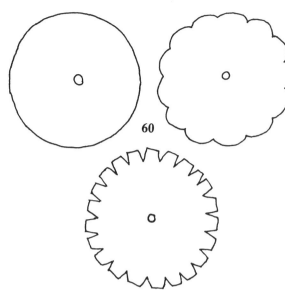

59

60

## FORGET-ME-NOT

For this flower, no specific materials are required. It is the simplest of all types of flower to make, being a single piece of flower-shaped material, and a central stamen. Any shape of petals – pointed, rounded, zig-zag, curved or simply disc shape – can be used (figs 59 & 60), and into the centre threaded one or more stamens. The flower shape can be flat or moulded, but, if a frilly one is required, crepe paper can be stretched to create undulations. The edges of flat organdie, silk, tissue paper, cut edge ribbon and paper can be curled.

For a cup-shaped disc it will be necessary to mould the centre either by stretching out the crinkles if crepe is used or by using a flower iron and pressing the fabric into a cushion to create a cup shape. Felt can be stretched in this way as well. Silk is a particularly effective material for these flowers especially when cut in various shapes and assembled in tiers. You may like to experiment with other shapes besides the ones in figures 59 and 60.

One way of emphasizing the edges is to dip the whole flower very lightly into a colour solution so that only the tips are tinted.

28

## FLORAL ALLIUM

61

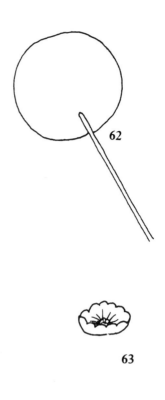

62

63

**Materials**
3.75 cm (1½ in.) diameter styrofoam ball
Approximately 36 forget-me-nots

Cover a stem wire with tape and insert it into the styrofoam ball with a little glue (fig. 62). Cut all the stems away completely from the forget-me-nots (fig. 63) and, starting at the top of the styrofoam ball, stick each one to it with a little glue. Continue in this way until the entire ball is covered with little flowers. This type of flower is, of course, very quick to make with ready made forget-me-nots. If these are unavailable, see previous page for forget-me-not instructions.

# WAX PAPER ORCHID

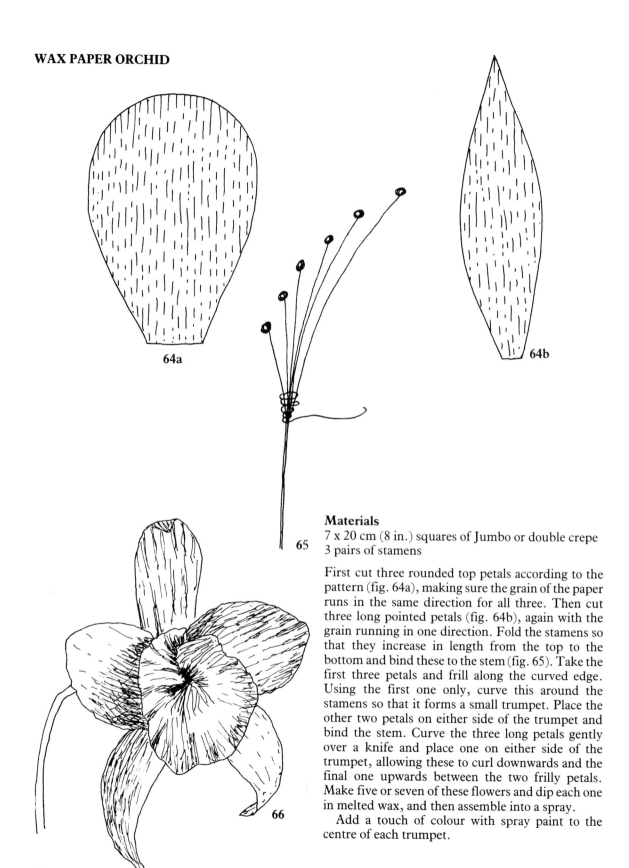

64a

64b

65

66

## Materials
7 x 20 cm (8 in.) squares of Jumbo or double crepe
3 pairs of stamens

First cut three rounded top petals according to the pattern (fig. 64a), making sure the grain of the paper runs in the same direction for all three. Then cut three long pointed petals (fig. 64b), again with the grain running in one direction. Fold the stamens so that they increase in length from the top to the bottom and bind these to the stem (fig. 65). Take the first three petals and frill along the curved edge. Using the first one only, curve this around the stamens so that it forms a small trumpet. Place the other two petals on either side of the trumpet and bind the stem. Curve the three long petals gently over a knife and place one on either side of the trumpet, allowing these to curl downwards and the final one upwards between the two frilly petals. Make five or seven of these flowers and dip each one in melted wax, and then assemble into a spray.

Add a touch of colour with spray paint to the centre of each trumpet.

30

# ORCHID SPRAY

## Materials
7 15 cm (6 in.) square single crepe paper

The orchid for this spray is identical to the wax paper orchid (*see previous page*) but single crepe paper is used. Crepe paper will not hold its shape when dipped in wax and so is best used for a delicate spray of tiny orchids.

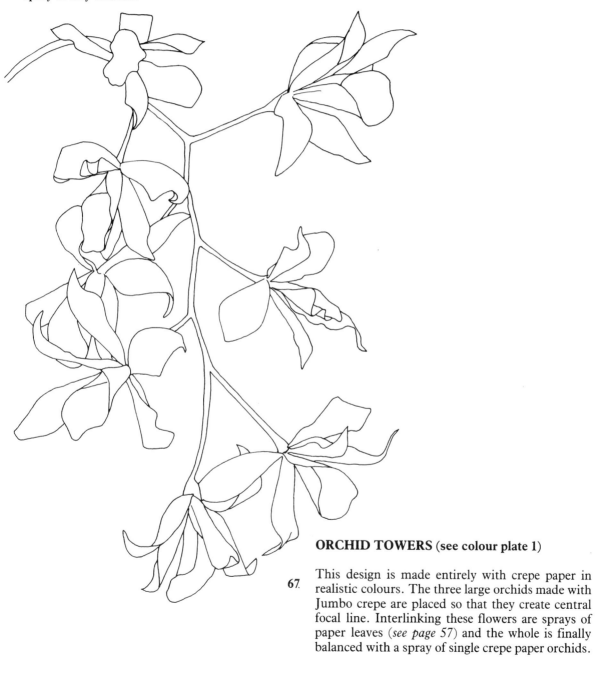

67

**ORCHID TOWERS** (see colour plate 1)

This design is made entirely with crepe paper in realistic colours. The three large orchids made with Jumbo crepe are placed so that they create central focal line. Interlinking these flowers are sprays of paper leaves (*see page 57*) and the whole is finally balanced with a spray of single crepe paper orchids.

31

# FELT ORCHID

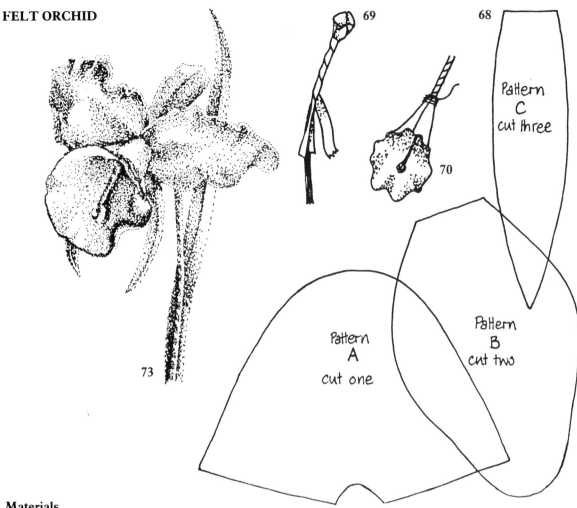

**Pattern C**
cut three

**Pattern A**
cut one

**Pattern B**
cut two

73

**Materials**
20 cm felt square
10 cm of 3 mm satin ribbon
5 stem wires

Tie a knot in the centre of the ribbon. Join the ends together and tape onto the stem wires (fig. 69).

Frill the curved edges of the fan-shaped petal (A) and join the straight edges with glue. Thread onto a stem and then bind with wire, allowing centre to show (fig. 70).

Frill the curved edges of the rounded petals (B) and press the middle into a cup shape. Pinching the straight end together, bind it to a stem so that it forms a triangle with the first petal (fig 71).

Fold each of the pointed petals (C) in half lengthways, stretching the fold to create a curve. Bind these petals to the stem, curving outwards in the spaces between petals (fig. 72).

Paint the base of the frilly petals, centre and edge of trumpet. Cover all visible wire.

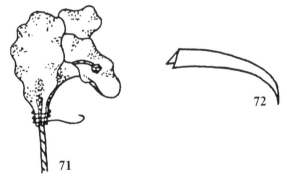

71

72

74

## FELT ORCHID SPRAY

This little spray is made with the felt orchid pattern opposite. The three smaller orchids are exactly half the size of the white one. Arch the stems of the smaller orchids, two to the right and one to the left and fix them just behind the main white orchid. Fill this area with ready-made silk begonia leaves, then cut thin strips of dark green felt to simulate orchid leaves. Join them together in loops and place these at intervals between other central material. Then complete the spray using multi-loop ribbon bows to cascade over the handle.

# SILVER BOUILLON ORCHID

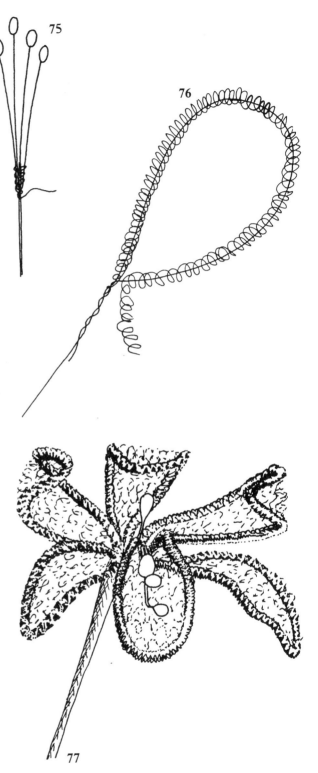

**Materials**
21 pairs pearl stamens
367.5 cm (147 in.) silver bouillon
42 rose wires

The instructions which follow are for one flower only, although the size of the complete plant is about the size of a Cymbidium orchid. You should therefore multiply the instructions to make up the spray.

Fold the three pairs of stamens in half and bind them to the stem (fig. 75). Stretch the bouillon very slightly, then take five rose wires and taking one of these thread it through the bouillon for approximately 10 cm (4 in.). Do not cut off the remaining bouillon. Join the free ends of the wire together by twisting them so that they form a loop, then pull out the springing from the bouillon and work this around the petals until a light cobweb of silver is created, then cut off the wire (fig. 76). Repeat this process with the other four rose wires. Take the first petal and coil it around the stamens so that it forms a trumpet then open out two of the wire loops so that they form rounded petals and place these diagonally on either side above the trumpet. Bind them together to the stem. Then pinch the remaining three petals together and curve them slightly so that they are long and thin. Bind these in the three spaces left by the first three petals. Ensure that these petals curl outwards then cover the wires with tape. Once you have made all the flowers, possibly five or seven, take a strong piece of wire or cane as the main stem and bind each one to it allowing each flower to have its own stem of approximately 7.5 cm (3 in.). Tape them so that each one just lies beneath the previous one. If you use a cane for this flower it will arch naturally because of the weight of the flowers.

34

# RIBBON CHRYSANTHEMUM

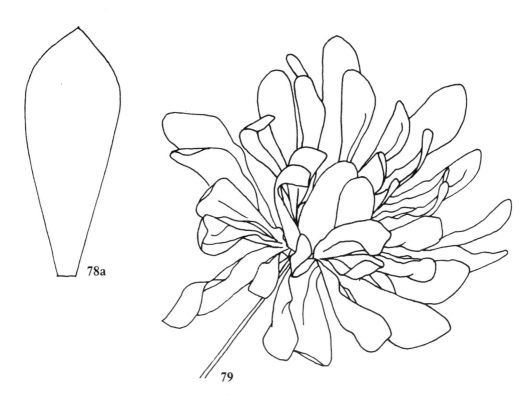

78a

79

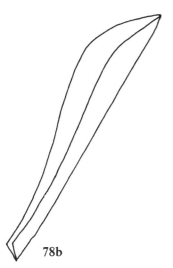

78b

**Materials**
247.5 cm (99 in.) 2 cm (¾ in.) wide cut-edge cotton ribbon
5 cm (2 in.) diameter cotton mould

Cut all the ribbon into lengths of 7.5 cm (3 in.) according to the pattern (fig. 78a). Fold each one in half lengthways and then, with a fingernail pressed into the tip of the petal, curl it away from the fold. Secure the cotton mould with glue to a stem wire. Then, working with all the petals curled inwards, glue a circle of petals around the cotton mould. Curl these a little more with a knife blade so that they curl right over the mould. They may not cover it in the initial circle, but as more are added the cotton mould should disappear altogether. Continue with circles of petals filling the spaces from the previous row each time until all the petals are assembled. The actual number of petals can vary according to the size of the chrysanthemum you require. Approximately thirty-three petals are needed. This chrysanthemum, although made here in cut-edge ribbon, is very effective with feathers and indeed they are made this way in Japan. Cartridge paper is also successful.

# BOUILLON FLOWER

# ARUM LILY

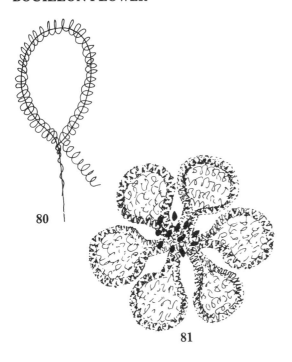

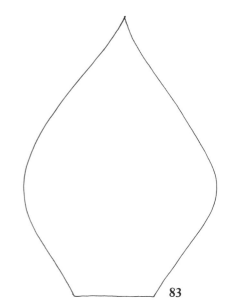

## Materials

1 pearl stamen
6 rose wires
25 cm (10 in.) bouillon

This is a traditional little flower from Austria where the bouillon, made in Liechtenstein, is extensively used with dried plant material.

Take one pearl stamen and bind it tightly to the top of a stem. Take one rose wire and thread 5 cm (2 in.) on to the wire, do not cut off remaining bouillon. Twist the ends of the wire together to trap the bouillon into a loop which is supported by the rose wire. Stretch out the springing in the bouillon from the base of the wire loop and then wind over and over this wire frame until a delicate cobweb is formed (fig. 80). Squeeze the wire into position, and cut off the remaining wire. Repeat this process with the other four rose wires until five petal shapes have been made. Attach the first one below the stamen and then the other five so that they radiate evenly around the centre. Cover the base of the petals and wires with tape and shape the petals so that they arch outwards from the centre.

Depending on your patience, this flower can be made with two rows of petals or even three; as an alternative centre, cloves can be used, first circled with a tiny wired loop of bouillon.

## Materials

15 cm (6 in.) chunky wool
10 cm (4 in.) square felt

Cut a piece of wool 15 cm (6 in.) long and bind this to the top of a stem wire covering approximately 10 cm (4 in.). Cover the end of the wool and the stem with tape. Then cut a piece of felt 10 cm (4 in.) square according to the pattern (fig. 83). Ease the felt out along the top of both sides so that it can curl outwards easily. Then coil this one shape around the woolly part of the stem so that the wool lies in the centre of this single-petalled flower. Cover the base of the petals and a little of the stem with more tape. If the coil shape of the arum lily does not stay together, secure with a little glue. The pointed profile often adds that essential touch of elegance to an otherwise somewhat rounded arrangement.

The arum lily can be made with any material which can be stretched, such as crepe paper, as indeed it could be made with metallic paper, tissue and organdie. It is not always essential to frill the edge of the petals, although the effect is considerably more realistic. As an alternative centre, any of the bulrush patterns, a stem of several beads on one or more wires, or dolls' hair used in place of the chunky wool would be suitable.

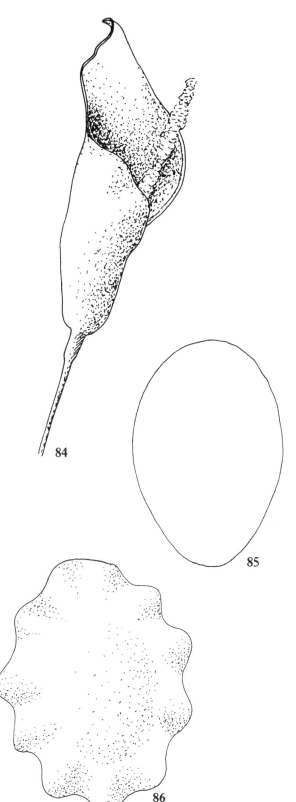

84

85

86

87

**Materials**
Eight 10 cm (4 in.) square felt
2.5 cm (1 in.) diameter styrofoam ball

Cut eight petals 10 cm (4 in.) square according to the pattern (fig. 85). Then stretch the edges of the petals until they become frilly and work the centre by easing the felt open to form a slight cup shape (fig. 86). When all the petals are shaped, fix the styrofoam ball at the top of a covered stem wire with glue. Work with the glue gun for this flower as it is a lengthy process with conventional tube glues. Take one petal and attach it half way up the styrofoam ball encasing the top completely. It may be necessary to add a little glue at this stage to the top of the ball so that the petals completely conceal the top of the styrofoam ball. Continue adding the remaining petals, overlapping each one by half until a frilly, open begonia appears. This is a large open flower which serves as an essential heavy focal point to a large arrangement. Any materials such as crepe paper can also be used here as they can be moulded to create the frilly petals. To emphasize the edge of the frills use spray paints or simply coat the edge with a brush or felt-tip pen.

## FELT OR PAPER POPPY

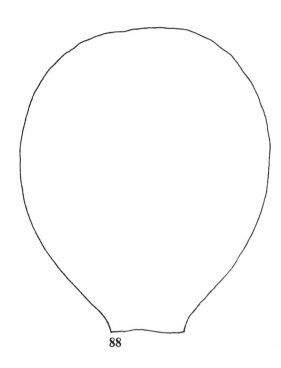

88

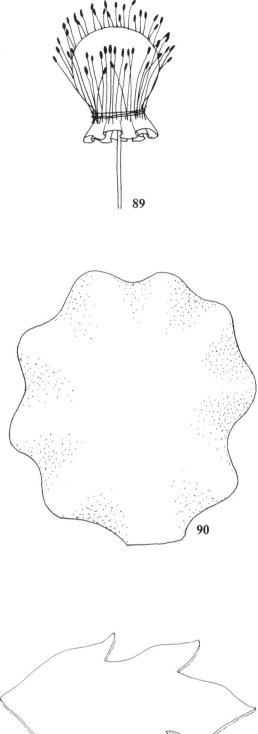

89

90

### Materials

20 x 40 cm (8 x 16 in.) felt
2.5 cm (1 in.) diameter styrofoam ball
¼ bunch of black stamens
7.5 cm (3 in.) black felt
Green felt for leaves

Cut eight petals 10 cm (4 in.) square according to the pattern (fig. 88). Glue the styrofoam ball to the top of the stem. Stretch the centre of the felt over the ball and bind it tightly underneath (fig. 89). Attach the stamens so that they radiate evenly around this centre (fig. 89). Take each petal and stretch the felt so that the edges undulate (fig. 90). Attach each petal separately, binding it to the centre making sure they are opposite each other so that four encircle the centre once and the second four are placed in the spaces between them.

For the leaves cut the felt according to the pattern (fig. 91) and gently pull each of the points of the leaves. Glue the wire through the centre of the leaf and tape it to the stem and then arch it outwards to begin with and then upwards so that it curls in towards the flower again. Crepe paper, particularly double crepe, is ideal for this type of poppy. For single Shirley poppies, where fewer frills are required, tissue paper creases a delicate effect.

91

# TISSUE PAPER POPPY

92

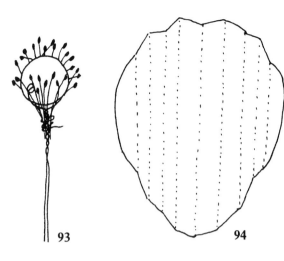

93

94

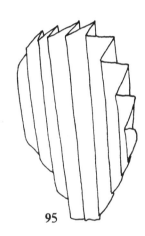

95

96

**Materials**
Tissue paper
1 black wooden bead
12 pairs black stamens

Thread the wooden bead with rose wire and bind this to the stem. Attach a circle of folded stamens around the bead (fig. 93).

Cut four tissue paper petals 7.5 cm (3 in.) long according to the pattern (fig. 94) and fold these petals vertically like a concertina (fig. 95). Bind two of the petals to the stem so that they face each other and then add the other two in the spaces.

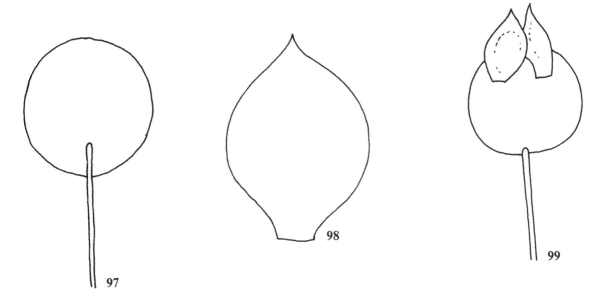

**Materials**
Flocked crepe paper
2.5 cm (1 in.) styrofoam ball

Bud
Attach the ball to the top of a stem wire (fig. 97). Cut
eighteen petals 2.5 cm (1 in.) square according to the
pattern (fig. 98), noting the direction of the grain.
Shape each of these petals by stretching the centre to
form a cup and curving the tip outwards. This will
give the petals a double curve. Take one petal and
apply with a little glue to the top of the styrofoam
ball and then, working round in a spiral, add each of
the petals separately by gluing (fig. 99). Continue in
this way until the complete ball is covered with
petals. All of the petals have the velvet on the outside
and are curved so that the tips lift away from the
centre of the bud itself.

Rose
Make a rose bud and then cut twelve petals 10 x 7.5
cm (4 x 3 in.) and glue them around the base of the
rose bud until you have made a full, open rose (fig.
101). If the velvet paper is not available, double
crepe is very effective for this flower as the two tones
in most types enhance the quality and both would be
visible as the tips of the petals curl outwards. For the
rose, the large additional petals should be cut from
the paper with the grain running in the opposite
direction so that when visible from the top all the
same colour is prominent.

101

## ROSE DESIGN

This design is made on a sheet of styrofoam which is covered with woven ribbon. Do this by sticking a row of ribbons along one side of the sheet. It is possible to use the glue gun, but be sure to put the glue onto the ribbon rather than onto the styrofoam so that the heat does not melt the foam. Then fix a second row of ribbon along one adjacent side, turn the foam over and weave the ribbons across each other before fixing the free ends again on the reverse side of the foam. Make one large velvet paper rose (*see page 40*) and three velvet paper rose buds, bind the three together into a spray and arch all the stems

over so that the flowers hang down. Make a spray of ten velvet tubing willows (*see page 27*), again arching the stems over. Tape these two sprays together so that the willow fills in the spaces between the flowers. Make five tubing leaves (*page 27*) before completing the whole spray by placing the big rose surrounded by the velvet tubing leaves at the base of the assembled spray of roses and willow. Thread this combined stem through the woven ribbon and arrange the leaves so that they support the whole design. Finally, trim the edge of the styrofoam base with the same tubing as the leaves.

# FELT DAHLIA

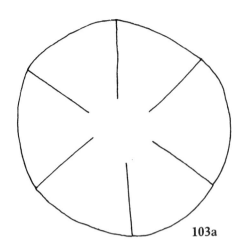

103a

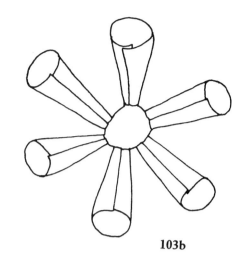

103b

## FELT DAHLIA

### Materials
Felt

Cut four 7.5 cm (6 in.) discs from the felt. Fold them in half and then in thirds so that you have a fan-shaped fold of felts. Cut the felt at each fold three quarters of the way along (fig. 103a). This will keep the centre intact when you open out the disc again. Take one segment and with a little glue coil the two side tips around and join them so that an open-ended cone is formed. Repeat this with each of the other five segments (fig. 103b). Take the stem wire and fold the top over and twist it into a knotted shape to prevent the petals falling off the top. Then thread each of the layers of petals through the centre onto the stem. Arrange the layers so that they are spaced and allow all the coils to be seen. Secure each layer with glue and then finally cover the stem with tape.

This particular flower would be effective if two layers of felt in two different shades were used for each petal. The result would be a two-tone dahlia. Any flat material, such as paper or stiff fabric, could also be used, but since the coil is the essential part it is really best to use a heavy fabric rather than a light one. For miniature dahlias, water-repellent cut-edge ribbon, particularly some of the patterned cotton types, would be effective and here again when two are used together (a patterned with a plain one) the coils would be most interesting.

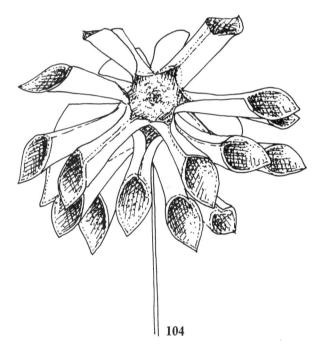

104

# FELT ROSE

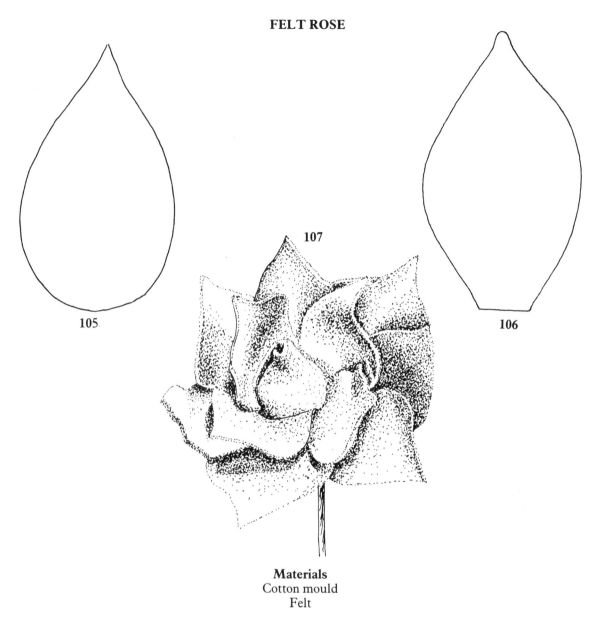

105

106

107

**Materials**
Cotton mould
Felt

Insert a covered wire into the cotton mould and secure with glue. Cut seventeen petals from the felt according to the pattern (fig. 105). Shape the felt by easing out the centre and stretching the top two sides so that they are allowed to curl outwards. They should curl away from the centre so that the petal has a double curved outline. Take the first petal, cut it off half way (fig. 106) and attach it to the centre of the side of the cotton mould with glue and then coil the top two sides together and join with glue so that this first petal is cone shaped to encase completely the top of the cotton mould. Continue with three more petals, again cutting the bases away and overlapping each one by half. These should form a tight coil of petals in the centre. Do not coil each one separately, but shape it round the first one. Continue adding petals and if necessary cut away the base of the petals each time. The rows of petals as they are added should gradually be worked down the remaining area of the cotton mould until the final petals are attached at the very base. This will allow them to open out in a realistic way. Felt is a heavy material and if you find that the petals fall down, it is always possible to apply a little glue to the previous layer which should retain the shape of the rose.

## WIRE FRAME PRIMROSE

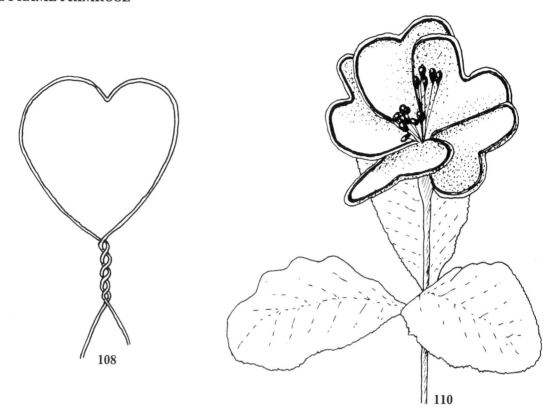

108

110

109

### Materials

Cotton or paper-covered wire
22.5 cm (9 in.) cut-edge satin ribbon (3.6 cm [1½ in.] wide)
22.5 cm (9 in.) green satin ribbon for leaves (3.6 cm [1½ in.] wide)
3 pairs of yellow stamens

First cut the covered wire into five lengths of 7.5 cm (5 in.). Join the ends of one and twist them together to form a loop and, pinching the centre, curve it inwards to form a heart shape (fig. 108). Repeat this with the other four pieces of wire. Apply a line of glue all round the edge of this shape and lay it flat onto the yellow ribbon and leave to dry. Attach the stamens to the stem (fig. 109) and then cutting away all surplus ribbon from the wire frame, bind these petals to the stem so that they radiate evenly from the centre. For the leaf, use a green covered wire 20 cm (8 in.) long and join the ends to form a loop and place this straight onto the ribbon. Cut away the extra material and bind this to the base of the primrose stem. As this flower has a wire frame, any material, light fabric or tissue paper is ideal, as indeed is plain wrapping paper.

# WIRE FRAME IRIS

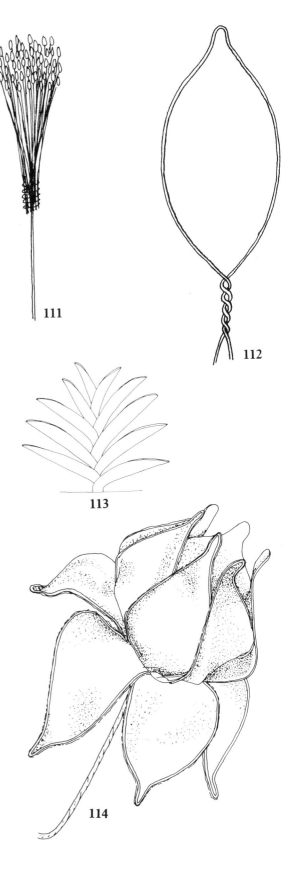

## Materials

14 pearl stamens
White cotton-covered wire
10 x 12 cm (4 x 12 in.) each of grey and lavender silk

Fold all the stamens in half and bind them tightly
with wire to the top of a stem with wire (fig. 111).
Cut twelve pieces of cotton-covered wire 30 cm
(12 in.) long and make a loop with each one by
twisting the ends together. Shape these into the
outline of the petal you require, according to the
pattern (fig. 112). Carefully apply a line of glue all
round the edge of the shape and then place it on to
the right side of the silk and allow it to dry. Cut away
any surplus material. You should make six of these
petals in one shade of silk and six in another shade.

Using the petals with the wire side uppermost,
take one of the petals of one shade and bind it tightly
to the stem binding point around the stamens. Add
the five others of the same colour to encase the
stamens once. The wires to these petals should be
facing inside the flower. Then add the second row of
petals with the wire facing the outside of the flower
until they have encased the other ones.

Now shape the iris by easing gently the inside
petals so that they curl right out and down beyond
the lower layer. Then shape the lower layer so that
each petal can stand up between its neighbour; these
are known as 'the falls'. Curve the tips of the petals
out slightly to make the centre more elegant and the
falls flow outwards slightly. This flower can be made
with virtually any fabric and in paper since the wire
frame not only stops the fabric fraying, but supports
the shape. Ribbon is particularly effective for this
flower.

The leaves, if you require them, should be made
of a material which does not fray, such as ribbon or
paper. Simply cut a long, straight, pointed shape,
fold it in half lengthways and attach with glue to the
base of the stem. For a full iris fan of leaves you
could simply repeat this process by adding leaves at
alternate sides and encase each one over the previous
one so that a fan results (fig. 113).

111

112

113

114

# WIRE FRAME CLEMATIS

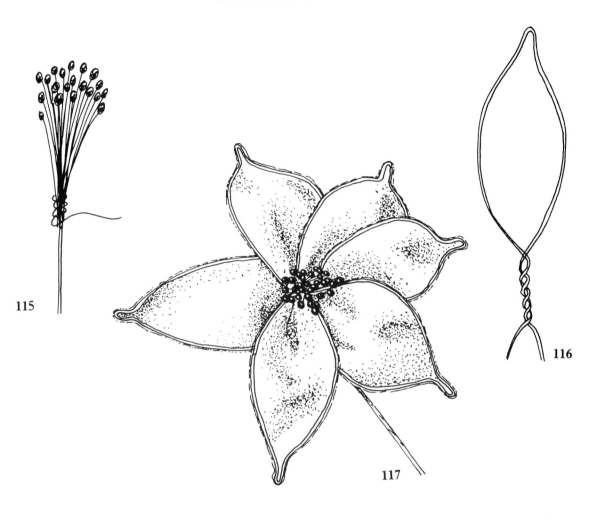

115

116

117

**Materials**
14 white pearl stamens
White cotton-covered wire
40 x 15 cm (16 x 6 in.) pale blue silk

Fold all the stamens in half and bind them to the top of the stem (fig. 115). Take the cotton-covered wire and cut it into six pieces 35 cm (14 in.) long and join each one into a loop by twisting the ends together (fig. 116). Shape this loop according to the pattern (fig. 117). Apply a thin line of glue carefully all round the edge of the wire and place it onto the silk. Repeat this with all the other pieces of wire and leave them on the silk until they are completely dry. Cut away all remaining surplus silk and shape the petals slightly by curving them and pinching the bases together so that the silk is allowed to undulate. Bind each one individually to the stem so that they radiate evenly from the stamens in the centre. Cover the binding and stem with tape. Shape the petals so that they arch out from the centre and then lift the tips slightly. This floating, saucer-shaped flower is ideal when a large area has to be covered, or indeed you need a centre of an arrangement filled. Since the wire frame will prevent any fraying and also support the shape of the petal many kinds of material can be used here. Organdie and net give a beautiful translucent appearance to the petals or alternatively you could choose ribbon, tissue paper and so on.

## ORGANDIE LILY SPRAY

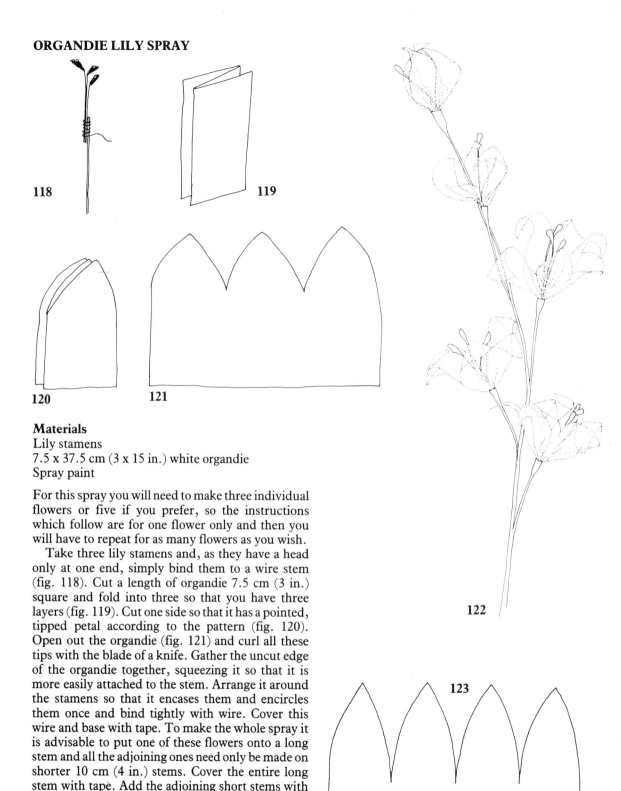

**118**

**119**

**120**

**121**

**122**

**123**

**Materials**

Lily stamens

7.5 x 37.5 cm (3 x 15 in.) white organdie

Spray paint

For this spray you will need to make three individual flowers or five if you prefer, so the instructions which follow are for one flower only and then you will have to repeat for as many flowers as you wish.

Take three lily stamens and, as they have a head only at one end, simply bind them to a wire stem (fig. 118). Cut a length of organdie 7.5 cm (3 in.) square and fold into three so that you have three layers (fig. 119). Cut one side so that it has a pointed, tipped petal according to the pattern (fig. 120). Open out the organdie (fig. 121) and curl all these tips with the blade of a knife. Gather the uncut edge of the organdie together, squeezing it so that it is more easily attached to the stem. Arrange it around the stamens so that it encases them and encircles them once and bind tightly with wire. Cover this wire and base with tape. To make the whole spray it is advisable to put one of these flowers onto a long stem and all the adjoining ones need only be made on shorter 10 cm (4 in.) stems. Cover the entire long stem with tape. Add the adjoining short stems with more tape. This double taping is to ensure that the sticky surfaces secure the angle of the stems.

1 *Orchid Towers*

**2** *Fireplace*

## ORGANDIE AZALEA

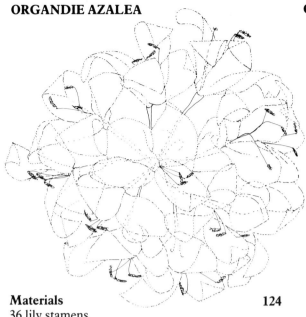

## ORGANDIE ANEMONE

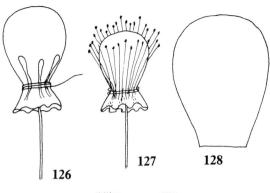

126    127    128

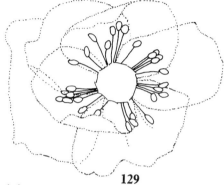

129

**Materials**                                    124
36 lily stamens
75 x 7.5 cm (28 x 3 in.) white organdie
Spray paint

This flower has a multiple head of little spray
flowers, so, referring to the instructions for the lily
spray (*see previous page*), make twelve flowers each
with four petals (fig. 123) and three stamens on 10
cm (4 in.) stems. Assemble the flower by joining all
the stems at exactly the same height to the main stem
which is essentially heavier gauge wire. It may be
necessary to support the weight of this flower by
adding more than one supporting stem.

When the flower is completely assembled, open
out the flowers so that they only just touch each
other to form a dome of tiny flowers. Finally, spray
very lightly with paint to help give texture and
emphasize the curls of the petals. This flower is
particularly effective with metallic papers at
Christmas and also cut-edge ribbon. Tissue paper
can, of course, be used as well as crepe paper.

**Materials**
2.5 cm (1 in.) diameter cotton mould
12 pairs pink stamens
80 x 10 cm (32 x 4 in.) white organdie
Pink taffeta

Cover the stem with tape and insert it into the cotton
mould, securing with glue. Place the taffeta over the
cotton mould and gather all the fabric underneath
the cotton mould and bind this tightly with wire (fig.
126). Then fold the stamens in half and, using
approximately three or four at a time, bind these
underneath the covered mould. By adding all the
stamens in a similar way they should encircle and
radiate from the centre (fig. 127). Cut six petals 10
cm (4 in.) square from the organdie according to the
pattern (fig. 128). Concertina fold the whole petal
lengthways, take each one separately and, holding
the base together, bind it tightly below the stamens.
Continue with all the remaining petals until the
whole area around the stamens is filled. Cover the
base of the petals and stem with tape. Spray with
metallic paint or another colour if you wish. This
little flower can also be made with paper or water-
repellent ribbon.

125

49

## SATIN BUD

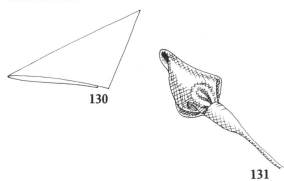

130

131

### Materials
5 cm (2 in.) square satin

Fold the piece of satin in half diagonally (fig. 130) and coil the two folded tips so that they overlap and by doing this a pointed cone will be formed. Gather the loose edges and bind them tightly to the flower stem (fig. 131). Cut away any surplus material and cover this with tape. This flower can be made equally well in crepe paper, ribbon, satin, organdie, in fact, in any fabric. It is ideal for patterned fabric or fabric which frays, as the raw edges are covered by the binding. Its unusual shape can lend contrast to the conventional round shape of a lot of flowers.

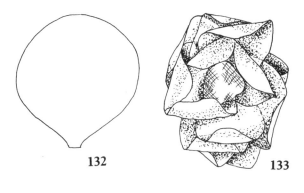

132

133

## SCENTED ROSE AND BUD

### Materials
Pot-pourri
30 x 10 cm (12 x 4 in.) white organdie
Spray paints

First cut a disc from the organdie 7.5 cm (3 in.) in diameter. Take a pinch of pot-pourri. Encase the pot-pourri inside the organdie disc by closing up the edges to form a little sack. Insert the wire stem with binding wire attached inside the pot-pourri and bind the edges of the organdie very tightly to the stem so that no pot-pourri is allowed to spill out. Cut six 5 cm (2 in.) petals according to the pattern (fig. 132). With the blade of a knife, curl each of the petals at the top. Take one of them and bind it tightly with the curve inwards over the centre. Add each of the other petals, making first a circle of three and then using the second three in the spaces for the second circle.

Cover the binding and stem with tape and spray the flower very gently with spray paint so that the white of the organdie adds a gentle contrast to the colour you have applied.

For the bud, make a centre in exactly the same way as the centre of the scented rose then cut four pieces of floral tape 2.5 cm (1 in.) long and twist the end of each one to form a point (fig. 134). Bind these overlapping at their bases to the pot-pourri sack. Twist these over the bud using a little glue in the centre. Cover the base with tape. Organdie has been chosen here for these flowers and buds becaue it allows the scent to escape. Alternative materials can be used, namely calico or cotton but not man-made fibre or any solid fibre, as the perfume will be lost.

To make matching leaves, cut tiny pointed leaf shapes from floral tape and put covered wire between two layers of leaves. Make sprays of five, one at the top with two pairs below.

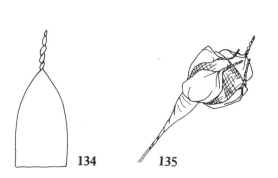

134

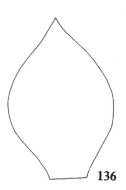

135

136        137

## TAFFETA ROSE (single and double)

## DAISY STEM

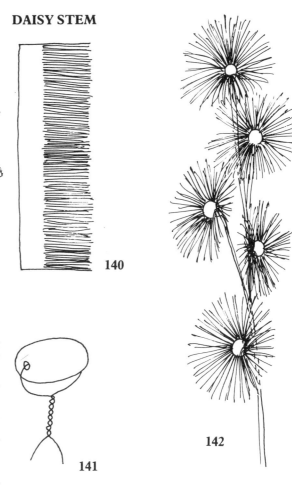

**138**

**139**

**140**

**141**

**142**

### Materials
Shot taffeta 53 x 7.5 cm (21 x 3 in.)

For the single rose cut five petals 7.5 cm (3 in.) long according to the pattern (fig. 136) and one oblong strip 5 x 12.5 cm (2 x 6 in.) and fray half of this (fig. 137). Attach this frayed strip to the stem by rotating the stem and gathering the piece as you go. This will form a trumpet shape rather than a tight roll. Take one of the rose petals and make a small pleat at the base of it to bind it to the rolled centre. Add each of the remaining four petals individually so that they each overlap the previous one slightly. Then carefully, with the blade of the knife, curl the tips of the petals outwards taking care not to create further fraying.

For the double rose, cut thirteen petals according to the pattern (fig. 136) and taking the first one, roll it tightly and attach to the stem. Then add the next one by pleating the base of it and binding it tightly. Each of the remaining petals should be added similarly overlapping each one by half and placing them so that each of the points arrive at different places and the whole flower is somewhat symmetrical when complete. This is a traditional rose pattern so it can be easily made with this material. Tissue paper is another good material for this flower and so are felt and organdie, indeed anything which you can mould with a knife without fraying.

To make the leaves for this rose, simply cut five pointed oval shapes and wire the back of each leaf. Assemble into a spray by taping one to the top of a stem and add the remaining four into two pairs one below the other.

### Materials
Two-tone taffeta (35 x 15 cm [14 x 6 in.])
7 silver beads

This consists of a stem of several little daisies. In fact, seven would be an appropriate number, but the instructions which follow are for one flower only. Cut an oblong piece from the taffeta 5 x 15 cm (2 x 6 in.) and fray half of this (fig. 140). Attach a bead to the top of a stem (fig. 141) then wrap the fabric around it so that the frayed part is the only area which is visible. As it is bound closely under the head this will press the material outwards radiating evenly from the centre. Repeat this process to make six other flowers and then tape one above the other to the stem. Arrange the flowers so that they are placed alternately on either side of the main stem.

## PAPER ORCHID

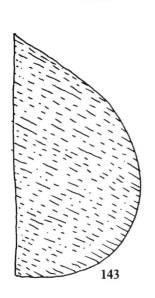

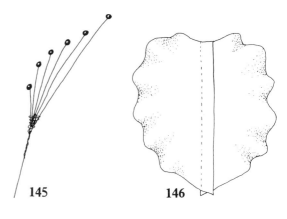

143

144

145

146

### Materials
45 cm (18 in.) square jumbo or duplex crepe
3 pairs yellow stamens
Spray paint

Cut six pieces 10 cm (4 in.) long from the crepe paper according to the pattern (fig. 143) all with the grain in the same direction. Then cut three pieces according to the second pattern (fig. 144), again with the grain in the same direction. Fold the stamens so that they lie in a line increasing in height and bind these to a stem (fig. 145). Take two of the first petal shapes and frill them along the curved edge (fig. 146). Glue these two together along the flat edge, overlapping them slightly. You will notice that the frilling causes the petal to curve so that when the two pieces are joined together no further wire is required to support them. Take the three narrow petals and curve these gently over a knife. Take the first petal and coil it round so that it encases the stamens and bind tightly. Place one of the other frilly petals to the top right-hand side of the first petal and the second one on the other side. Shape the petals so that these two top ones curl away from the first one. Take the curved petals and place them in the three spaces provided by the first ones. The top petal should point upwards and curl away from the centre, the last two petals should curl downwards on either side of the original trumpet petal. Finally, with a short sharp spray add an additional touch of colour to the centre of the trumpet.

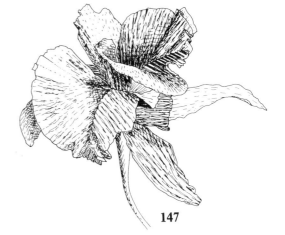

147

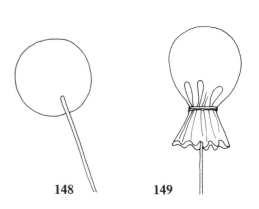

148

149

# CREPE PAPER ANEMONE

# GOLD GENTIAN

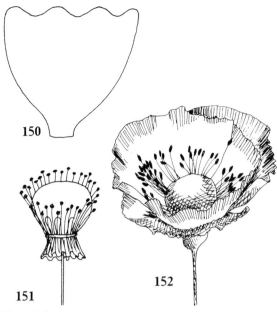

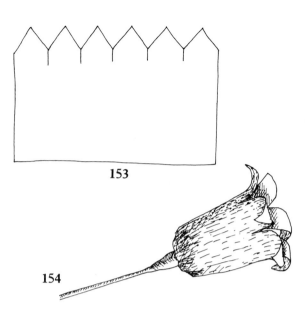

## Materials

Cotton mould 1 cm (½ in) diameter
Black single crepe paper 5 cm (2 in.) square
24 pairs black stamens
Cream jumbo crepe 60 x 7.5 cm (2 ft x 3 in.)

Attach the cotton mould to the stem with glue (fig. 148). Then take the black crepe paper and stretch the centre slightly before placing it over the cotton mould. Gather the edges of the crepe paper into the stem and bind tightly with wire (fig. 149). Cut a strip of cream crepe paper across the fold so that the crinkles in the opposite direction to the strip that has been cut, then dip this strip into a glass of diluted paint and allow to dry. During the drying process, the crinkles will open out and the paint will run down at irregular intervals into the paper giving a gentle outline for the petals.

When completely dried (this should take approximately twenty-four hours) cut eight petal shapes according to the pattern (fig. 150). Before placing the petals into position, fold all the stamens in half and bind them in groups of four at the same binding point. They should radiate evenly all round the paper-covered centre (fig. 151). Take one of the petals, ease the centre out very lightly and pleat the base of the petal together before binding at the binding point. Add each of the remaining petals by a similar process, making first a circle of four petals before adding a second circle of four in the spaces between the original ones. Finally, cover all binding with tape.

## Materials

Metallic gold crepe paper 15 x 7.5 cm (6 x 3 in.)

This flower could have gold stamens in the centre if you wish, but as the simple bell shape is normally seen from the side, stamens are really not essential.

For the bells, fold the paper into half three times and cut one side into little points; this will create a strip of six petals (fig. 153). With the blade of a knife curl all the tips outwards. At this point you could decide whether the gold should be visible on the outside or the inside of the flower. The curls of the tip go towards the outside. Then coil the strip around, joining the end to the beginning and squeezing the uncurled edge of the petal in together tightly over a finger so that it forms a good shoulder opening the base of the bell shape flower. Then insert the wire stem and bind tightly with binding wire. Cover all the wire and the base of the petal with tape.

## ROLLED PAPER ROSE

### Materials
Crepe paper

Any crepe paper, from the single, double to the jumbo are all perfectly suitable for this little flower, as indeed is foil crepe.

Cut a strip 10 x 5 cm (4 x 2 in.), noting the direction of the grain (fig. 155). Join the end to the top of a stem and roll it gently so that it spirals into a tube. Rotate the stem slightly and roll this tube around the stem and join the end of it to the stem to finish off. The size of the flower depends upon the number of times the paper encircles the stem.

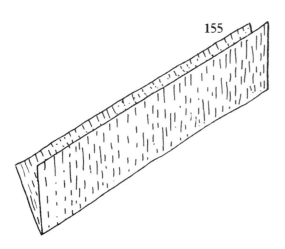

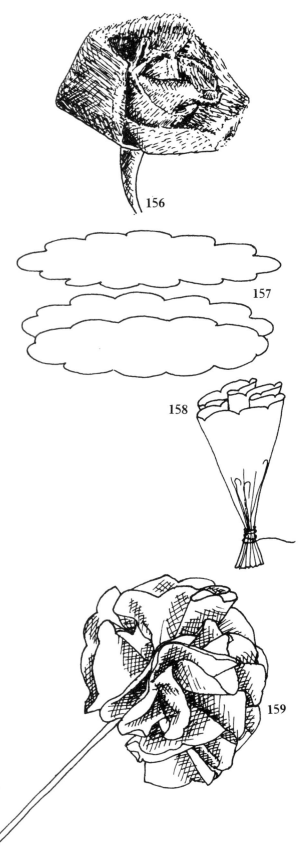

### COASTER CARNATION

### Materials
1 coaster

This carnation was inspired by the paper coasters which can be bought in stationery shops.

Separate one of these coasters and discover how many layers there are (fig. 157). There will be approximately eight layers. Take one layer, pinch it together in the centre and bind this to the top of a stem (fig. 158). Continue adding layers until the flower has reached the size you require. Approximately eight layers are used, but if you require smaller flowers then naturally four or six should be sufficient. An interesting texture can be added with metallic spray paint if you are to use this flower in a Christmas arrangement. Spray very lightly so that only the tips of the petal have added colour.

# FEATHER LILY

160

161

162

**Materials**

Goose satin feathers
3 pairs stamens

Choose the feathers carefully, making sure that they are all from the same side of the bird so that they will curl in the same direction. Also make sure that they are the soft satin feathers and not the stiffer ones which tend to grow higher up in the wing.

Use a large pair of scissors, cutting boldly the edge of the feather so that you can form a pointed petal shape (fig. 160). Use the blade of a blunt knife easing the feather over gently so that the tip curls. Bind the three pairs of stamens to the top of a stem (fig. 161) and add the petals individually so that they radiate evenly from the centre.

Variations on this lily can be interesting. Exotic versions with layers and layers of feathers are beautiful and fronds of peacock and ostrich feathers can be intermingled with the stamens. As an alternative, strip away the base of some of the stiffer satins cut them and curl the tips and use these in place of the stamens. Also chicken hackle feathers make a good combination with satins in the centre. The circles of curled feathers should always be in multiples of six. If two layers are used, interesting colour combinations can be created by using one circle of one colour and then a second circle of another.

55

# GRAPES

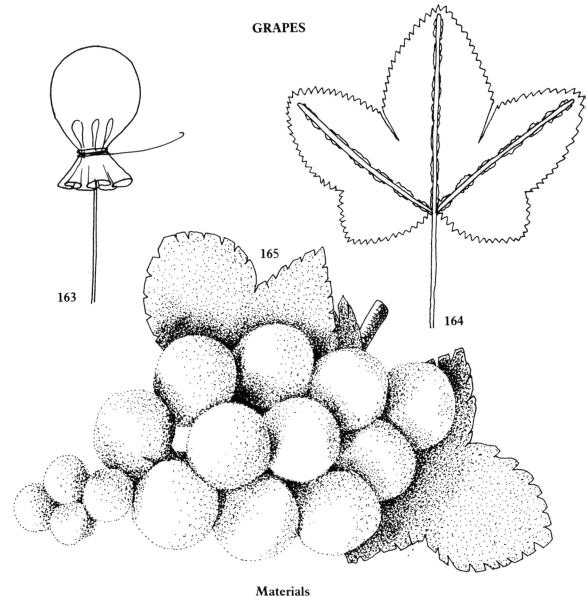

**Materials**
45 cm (26 in.) butter muslin
13 cotton moulds 1.5 cm (½ in.) in diameter
Spray paint
Felt for leaf

Fix each of the cotton moulds on to individual stems. Then cut thirteen pieces of butter muslin 5 cm (2 in.) square and cover each one and bind tightly with wire (fig. 163). Be sure to cut away as much of the material underneath as possible to prevent the binding being bulky. Assemble the spray of grapes by taping them all together so that they form a long pointed triangle. Spray with paint, making sure that all surfaces are covered.

With a piece of felt cut a vine leaf shape and glue a wire to the back (fig. 164). Make three of these leaves and bind them tightly to the stem of the spray. They should enhance the top and finish off the whole shape.

These grapes can be made with any material. The heavier ones being preferable with large cotton moulds. Or, for miniature grapes, wooden beads would be ideal. Satin is a good material to use as the shine gives an extra dimension.

## ARTIFICIAL GRASS PAPER LEAVES

### Materials
Artificial grass paper

Although artificial grass paper is used here, virtually any type of paper can be used. Cut an oval pointed shape and bind this to the top of a stem.

## WOOLLY LEAF

### Materials
Textured knitting wool

The texture of the wool is important here as it lends interest to what would otherwise be simple wool-covered wire. The leaf is made in five parts so use five separate stub wires 1 ft long. Bind each one with wool and join the ends together to form a loop. Arrange them in a fan so that the two on either side of the base are slightly smaller than the three above them. This woolly leaf can also be made with chenille or tinseltex, giving a different effect.

166

167

## PAPER LEAVES

168

169

170

171

### Materials
Single crepe paper
Double crepe paper
Jumbo crepe paper

The patterns here (figs 168-171) can be adapted to any form of leaf. To wire the leaf, run a line of glue down the centre of the leaf, place the wire on the glue and fold the leaf in half. Open the leaf out again. The wire will be encased in paper forming a ridge which looks like a natural vein to the leaf. For the spray, attach one leaf to the end of a long stem and then add leaves in pairs down the stem, arching each leaf out slightly. Lime green crepe paper is used to make a realistic variegated leaf with the centre painted a deep green. For the long leaf fan, make each leaf separately and then tape the leaves together bending the wire to form the arched shape.

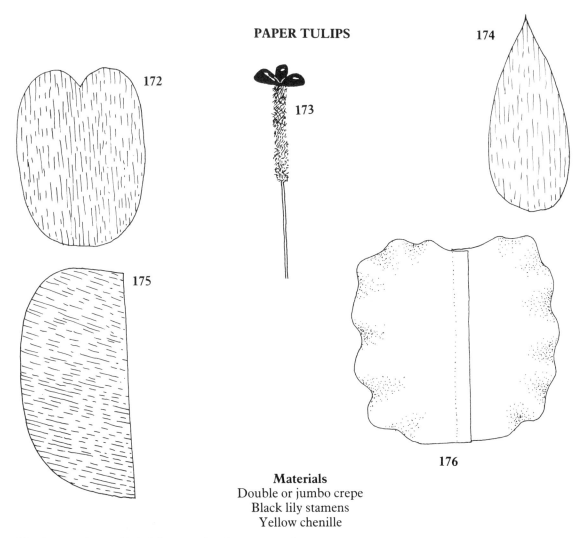

**Materials**
Double or jumbo crepe
Black lily stamens
Yellow chenille

The instructions which follow are for three types of tulips. For the Darwin tulip (fig. 177) you will need red crepe paper. Cut six petals according to the pattern (fig. 172) 10 cm (4 in.) long, noting the direction of the grain. Bind three lily stamens together using the chenille so that only the heads are visible and press the heads so that they point outwards. Bind this to the stem (fig. 173). Wire the tulip petals by applying a line of glue to the centre of the petal. Put the wire on to the glue and fold the petal in half. Then open it out again and use this wire support to shape the petal. Attach three petals, first to the stem and then three more in the spaces provided. Curve them all deeply at the base so that they open out away from the centre, then straighten the sides, curving only the tip of the petals inwards at the top.

For the second tulip, with pointed petals (fig. 178), cut six petals according to the pattern (fig.

174). Make the centre in the same way as the first one. Wire each of these six petals and attach three of them to form a circle with three more in the spaces provided. Curl these petals gently outwards and upwards allowing the tips to curve out again at the top.

For the third type of tulip, the Parrot tulip (fig. 179), make the centre in exactly the same way as for the first two types of tulip. Cut twelve pieces of crepe paper, watching very carefully the direction of the grain. Apply a line of glue down the straight edge of one piece (fig. 175), put the wire on top of this glue and the second piece on top of that so that it goes in the opposite direction. Frill along the curved sides of this petal (fig. 176). Make the other five petals by the same process. Attach three of these petals to the stem then three more in the spaces. Curve these petals so that they form a rounded tulip shape, curling them in at the top.

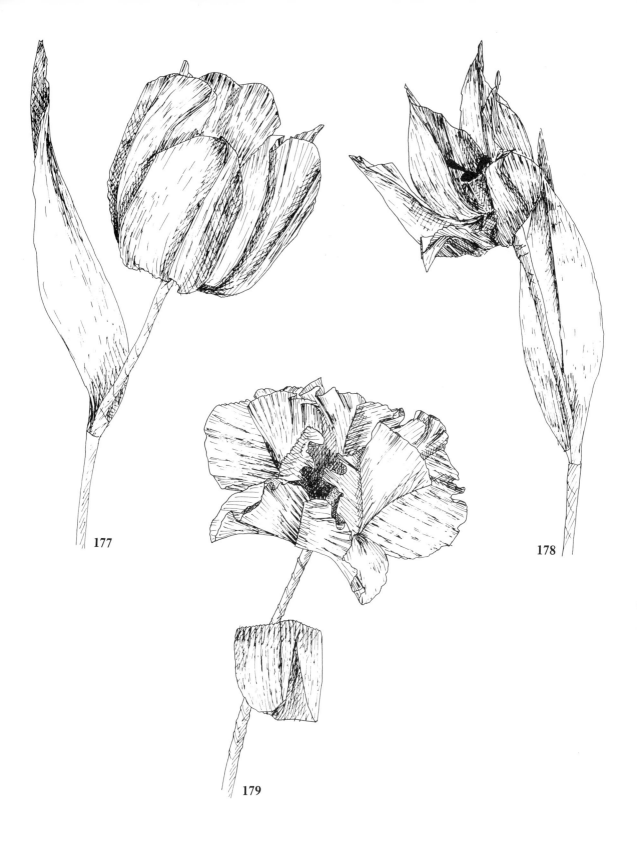

177

178

179

59

## PAPER WATER LILY

180

181

## PAPER FUCHSIA

182

183

184

### Materials

1 roll 10 cm (4 in.) wide double crepe paper or
jumbo crepe paper

For this flower double crepe paper, foil crepe or
jumbo are all suitable. First cut one strip according
to the pattern straight across the roll of crepe paper
so that you have a row of pointed petals with a solid
base (fig. 180). Take the first strip and pinch it
tightly together at the base and bind it to the stem.
Continue with each of the remaining strips until all
are assembled. For wax water lilies make this flower
and dip it into melted candle wax, ensuring that the
base of the petals and stem are also coated so that the
flower is waterproof.

### Materials

Duplex or jumbo crepe paper
Four pairs of stamens

Cut one strip of the crepe paper with four points
according to the pattern (fig. 182) and a second one
simply oblong which should be frilled all along one
of the long sides (fig. 183). Join the stamens to the
stem and then pinch together the frilled piece of
crepe paper and bind it to the stem so that the
stamens protrude above the frilly edge of the paper.
Ensure that this paper encircles the stem only once
and bind tightly. Repeat the process with the strip of
pointed petals and then curl the tips of each of these
outwards. Cut the leaves from the pattern (fig. 184).
This fuchsia can be made with feathers, felt, many
different kinds of paper, organdie and silk.

This is a very versatile flower which is easily
recognisable whatever size it is made and whatever
material is used. It is ideal where pendant flowers or
profile flowers are required in an arrangement (fig.
185).

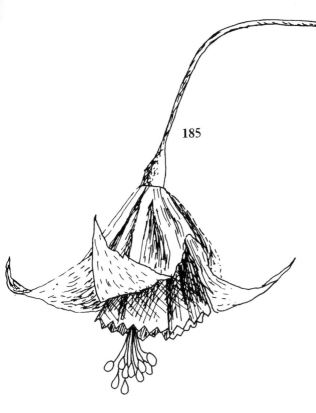

185

186

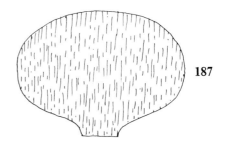

187

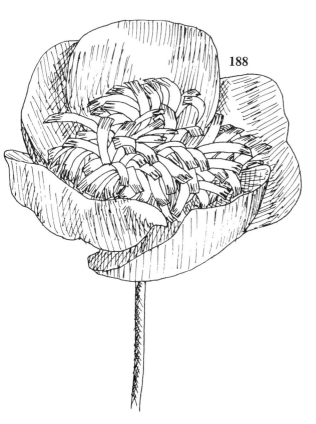

188

## Materials

Duplex crepe paper

Cut three strips 15 x 5 cm (6 x 2 in.) according to the pattern (fig. 186) and form them into cones. Then cut five rounded shapes 7.5 cm (3 in.) tall (fig. 187). Note carefully the direction of the grain on both these shapes. Curl all the tips of the cone-shaped strips and, taking the rounded petals, ease the centre out so that they become dome shaped. Take one of the cone-shaped strips and roll it with the curls curling outwards. Attach this roll to the top of a stem. Repeat this with the other two strips so that the curls tumble over each other when all three rolls are attached. Then take one of the rounded petals and bind this so that it cups the curly centre. Continue with the other four petals until they encircle the centre completely. It may be necessary when the flower is completed to ease out these domed petals even further so that the cup is more acute. Spray the entire flower very lightly with paint.

## PAPER ZINNIA

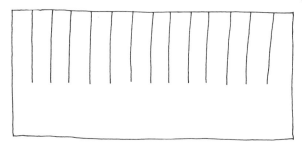

**189**

**190**

**191**

**Materials**
One cotton mould
Crepe paper

Cut a strip from the roll of crepe paper while it is still intact 7.5 cm (3 in.) wide and cut into this strip according to the pattern (fig. 189), making a cone-shaped row of petals 1.25 cm (½ in.) wide. Stretch the crepe paper at the top of all the petals, which will curl them round, then attach the cotton mould to the top of the stem (fig. 190) and gather this strip of petals around the cotton mould binding with wire as you go. As a final touch of colour spray lightly with paint. Any form of crepe paper can be used for this zinnia. In fact, a mixture of two or three different tones of one colour, particularly in single crepe or a layer of glass crepe between the solid ones, would be effective.

## RIBBON ROSE

### Materials
Size 9, 36 mm (1½ in.) wide cut-edge satin

The instructions which follow are for a single rose, which is normally made with one ribbon, but it is made here with two to show clearly where the ribbon is folded over.

192-211

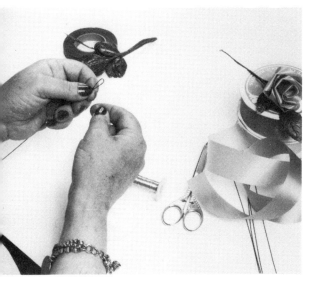

**Stage 1** Attach the binding wire to the stem and make a hook in the top.

2 Place the ribbon in the same direction as the wire on the left-hand side of the hook. Rotate the stem clockwise with the left hand, holding the binding wire across the ribbon.

3 Continue rolling until all the ribbon is secure.

4 Bend the ribbon over the hook away from you.

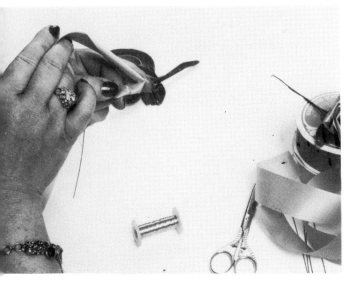

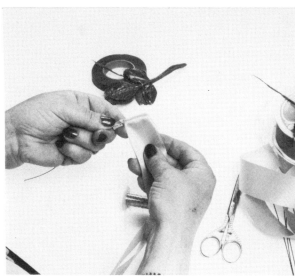

**5** Bring the ribbon round so that it passes the front.

**6** Continue binding the ribbon three or four times until a tight roll is achieved.

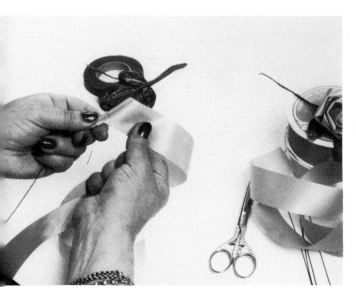

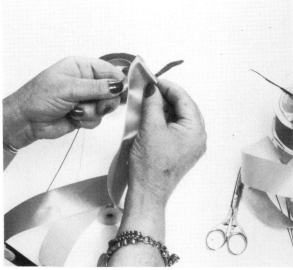

**7** Lift the ribbon diagonally upwards.

**8** Fold the ribbon diagonally out towards you.

64

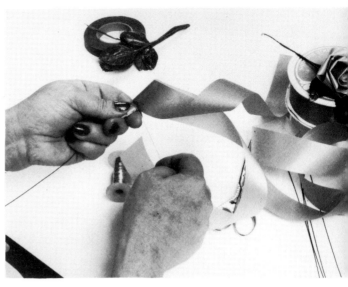

**9** Lift the binding wire over to catch the side of the ribbon.

**10** Rotate the stem clockwise holding the wire tight in the process and at the same time ease the ribbon upwards again.

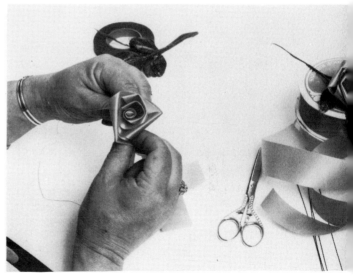

**11** Make another fold diagonally towards you.

**12** Continue repeating this process, watching that all the folds are level at the top and that they are placed at irregular intervals.

**13** When you reach the end of the ribbon gather it together.

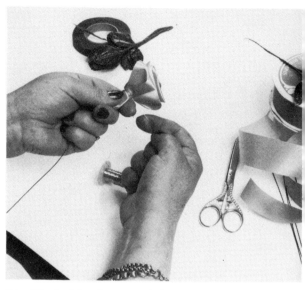

**14** Bind with wire several times around this end to secure it.

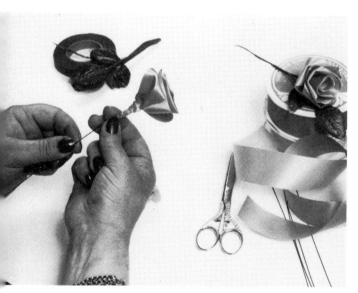

**15** Continue with the binding wire until all the ribbon is secured. The binding will have worked down the stem.

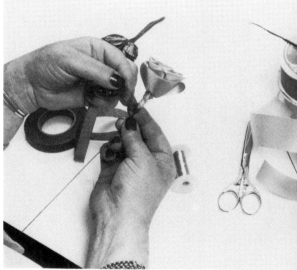

**16** Start taping the rose at the base of the ribbon and work upwards towards the flower.

**17** Continue taping the base of the flower until the wire binding is well covered.

**18** Work down the stem with the tape and place a leaf spray beside the stem.

**19** Continue taping both stems together.

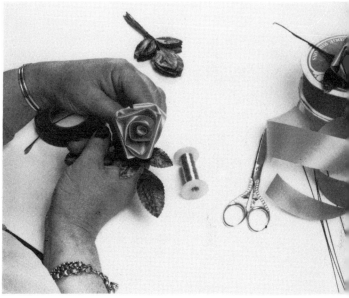

**20** The finished rose should sit on a spray of leaves and when visible from the top should reveal layers of rotating folds.

Use cut-edge ribbon when you first start making roses as the water-repellent substance, being reasonably stiff, is easier to handle and retains the folds, but for the advanced rose maker any ribbon is possible and any width. Simply vary the length of ribbon you use, for example, 30 cm (1 ft) of 2.2 cm (1 in.) ribbon or 1 m (3 ft 3 in.) of 4.4 cm (2 in.).

## SATIN ROSE

**Materials**
Slipper satin
Iron-on vylene
Organdie

Start the centre of this rose by making a ribbon rose bud (*see page 63*). Then cut eleven petals out of all three materials according to the pattern (fig. 213). Iron the satin onto the vylene to stiffen the material and also to prevent fraying. Then, using milliners' wire, glue one to the centre of the back of each petal. Glue one shaped organdie petal on the top of each satin one, curving the edges of each side outwards. They should undulate gently over the satin ones which can be shaped with the supporting wire. Take three petals first and bind them to the satin bud with

the right sides outwards and shape the satin part of these so that they curve in over the buds and the petals lift upwards gently. Then add each one following individually so that all the petals lie within the spaces of the other ones. This is a very large flower which can be displayed individually on a velvet-covered spiral stem and in which case artificial rose leaves should be added to fill the stem area. If it is to be used as a corsage or on a hat, the leaves should really radiate from the flower head just below the stem.

# TAPED ROSE BUD

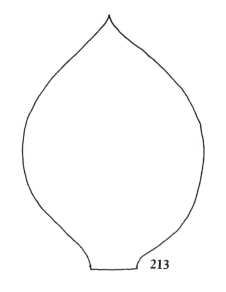

213

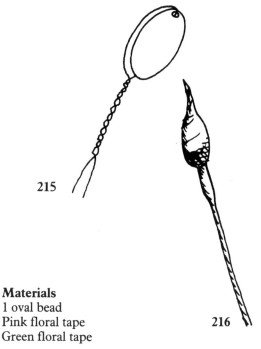

215

216

214

**Materials**
1 oval bead
Pink floral tape
Green floral tape

First thread the bead onto a stem wire, bending the top of the wire, and twist it to the original stem, thus encasing the bead (fig. 215). Using the pink floral tape, cover this bead extensively, finishing with a twist of pink tape at the top of the bud. With green tape, simply cover the stem (fig. 216).

This little bud is very useful when the tiny points are required. The choice of colour for the bud can then be selected to match those of the flowers. If a fatter bud is required then a round bead would create the shape for you.

## CHENILLE TENDRIL

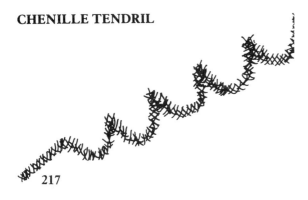

**217**

### Materials
1 stem chenille

This simple but effective tendril is made by winding one stem of chenille around a pencil so that it forms a spiral. This can be stretched out until the required length is achieved. Different sizes of tendrils can be made by varying the article around which the chenille is bound. For example, for miniature work the tiny stems of artificial leaves can be bound around a needle.

## RIBBON HOLLY LEAF

### Materials
15 cm (6 in.) 5 cm (2 in.) wide cut-edge satin ribbon
Tinseltex chenille

Simply cut a holly leaf shape according to the pattern (fig. 218a) from the ribbon, apply a line of glue along the length of the leaf on the right side and attach the tinseltex allowing any remaining to form the stem (fig. 218b).

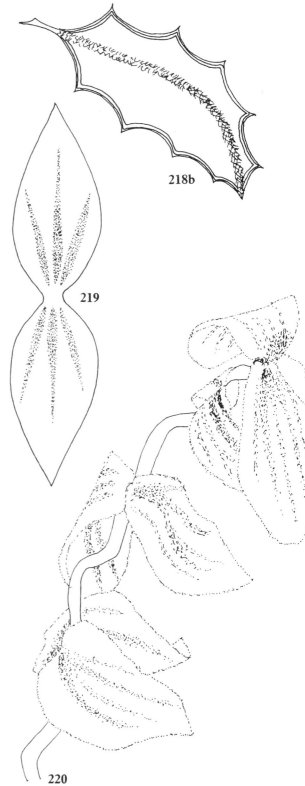

**218b**

**219**

**220**

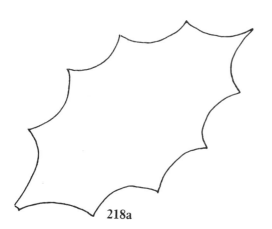

**218a**

## FELT TRADESCANTIA

### Materials
White felt
White plastic tubing

Cut approximately forty-two leaves according to the pattern (fig. 219). These are double leaves. Take two leaves and twist milliners' wire around the ends to form a pair, then bind this to the top of a long stem wire and insert into a length of white plastic tubing. Make a kink in the stem wire to secure the position of this pair of leaves. A little below this, cut a notch in the plastic tubing and make another pair of leaves by the same process and insert this into the slit in the tubing. A notch just below this pair of leaves will secure this position also. Repeat the process until all the stems (seven of them) are filled with leaves. Mark the leaves with green crayon in lines radiating from the centre. Arrange the stems together and place them in a container so that they arch upwards as if to imitate a trailing plant.

221

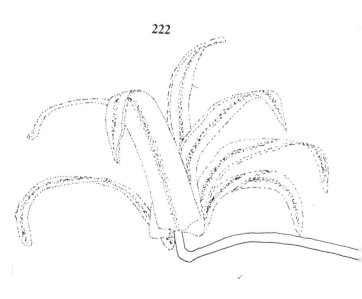

222

## SPIDER PLANT

### Materials
Green felt
Green paint
Plastic tubing

Cut eighteen long, thin, pointed pieces of felt of varying lengths, the longest being 40 cm (1 ft 4 in.) and the shortest being 20 cm (8 in.) long. Then cut thirteen more long thin pointed strips 7.5 cm (3 in.) and mark all these strips with green paint in stripes, irregularly along their length (fig. 221). Take some green, covered wire (milliners' wire is the best) and glue this to the back of every leaf. Make a bunch of seven small leaves and bind them to the top of a long heavy stem wire. Insert into the plastic tubing. Then make a bunch with the remaining six small leaves and repeat the process. Join these two long stems together with a bunch of all the remaining leaves and bind them all together tightly. Curve all the leaves outwards and arrange them so that the two small ones appear to spring from the central roots.

## PLANTS 223

Combinations of plants in a jardinière make an interesting and welcome change from traditional floral designs.

## METALLIC LILY

### Materials
Prism foil
10 pairs silver holly berries

Cut all the metallic foil into shapes according to the pattern (fig. 224) 10 cm (4 in.) long and make a hole in the base of each one. Take the silver holly berries, leaving two pairs aside, and fold them in half and bind to the top of a stem wire (fig. 225). Take the two remaining pairs and bind them tightly so that the berries cover the binding which secures the bunch. Thread all the petals onto the stem below the berries and secure with tape by binding several times below the petals. Be sure always to cut the petals across the roll of paper; this will ensure a gentle curve which the strength of the material will retain without need for support.

## DUTCH FLOWER PAINTING (see facing colour plate)

Inspired by the work of Dutch artists in their still life paintings, this kaleidoscope of flora is fun to make because you can use any material available when an assortment of colour schemes is needed. It has the added advantage of having only one or two of each flower. Contained in this one you will find: one velvet paper rose; two tarlatan peonies; two paper arum lilies; two crepe paper anemonies; two paper fuchsias; one wire frame iris; two wire frame clematis; one tarlatan lily; four ribbon roses; five various tulips (some of them painted); one organdie azalea; two tarlatan carnations; two tissue paper poppies; two scented organdie roses (made entirely of organdie petals); two wood fibre daffodils; two crepe paper peonies; one paper water lily; one wax water lily; one satin rose; one organdie lily spray; one felt poppy.

These flowers are combined with paper leaves, felt tradescantia and poppy leaves and completed by a bunch of grapes, resting on the table.

**3** *Dutch Flowers*

**4** *Scented Spray*

**5** *Purple Dome*

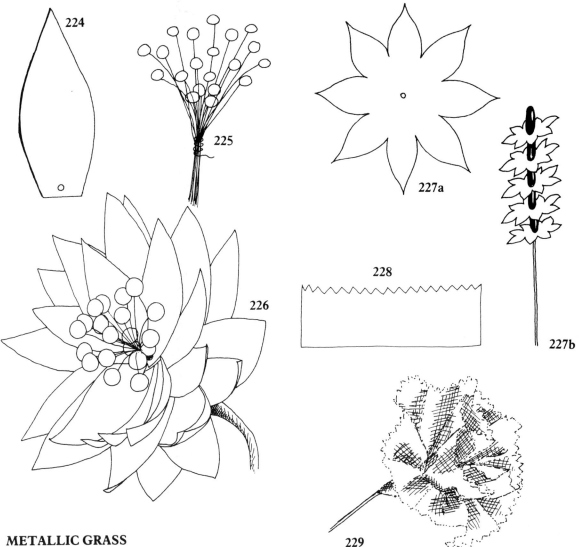

224

225

227a

226

228

227b

229

## METALLIC GRASS

### Materials
Metallic prism foil
18 oval wooden beads

Cut the metallic foil into seventeen pieces according to the pattern (fig. 227a) 3.5 cm (1½ in.) in diameter and make a hole in the centre of each one. Start by threading a rose wire through the centre of one bead and twist this to the top of a stem wire. Cover the entire stem with tape and thread alternately one layer of flower disc and then one layer of bead until all the materials are threaded (fig. 227b). Cover the remaining stem again with tape to secure the position of the beads and flowers. Ordinary acetates and plastic sheeting are also suitable, as well as stiffened papers. Crepe, however, cannot be used as it will not hold a shape without support.

## TARLATAN CARNATION

### Material
Tarlatan

Cut a strip of tarlatan 70 cm (28 in.) long from a piece you have previously sprayed with colour and trim one of the long sides with pinking shears (fig. 228). Start with one end and gather this to the top of a stem. Continue binding and gathering until all the material is secured around the stem. With care, this should radiate evenly and produce a frilly flower (fig. 229). Very many different materials can be used for this simple gathered type of carnation, including ribbons and paper.

73

## TARLATAN TIGER LILY

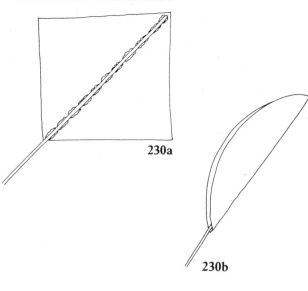

230a

230b

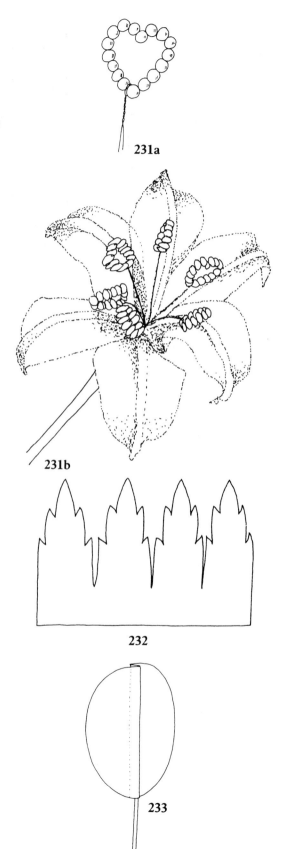

231a

231b

232

233

**Materials**
Tarlatan
Six heart-shaped pearl rings
Cotton-covered wire

Cut the tarlatan into six pieces 10 cm (4 in.) square
and the cotton-covered wire into six lengths 15 cm
(6 in.). Apply a line of glue diagonally across one of
the squares and place the cotton-covered wire on this
line (fig. 230a) and fold the tarlatan in half
diagonally whilst the glue is still sticky (fig. 230b).
When the glue has dried cut the open sides into half
of the rounded petal and then open out these layers
so that the full petal is visible and shape it by curling
it over starting from the tip of the petal. Repeat this
process with the other five squares of tarlatan. Take
one of the heart-shaped pearl rings and thread a rose
wire through the base of it, twisting the ends
together to form a stem (fig. 231a); repeat this
process with the other five hearts. Make a bunch of
six hearts and stamens together, binding them to the
top of a stem and allowing their own stems to extend
about 5 cm (2 in.). Then attach the petals so that the
tips curl outwards by placing three on first and then
the second three in the spaces provided by the first
ones. This is a plain tiger lily, but a splash of paint
could be added to the centre. This is done by
dipping a toothbrush into paint which is first diluted
with water and then flicking the colour into the
centre of the lily. This produces a natural random
spotted centre which you can build up as much as
you wish.

## TARLATAN PEONY

234

**Materials**

Tarlatan
Milliners' wire

Cut four strips of pointed petals according to the pattern (fig. 232) 10 x 10 cm (4 x 4 in.) and cut five oval petals 12.5 cm (5 in.) long. Take one of the strips of pointed petals and roll and bind to the top of a stem wire. Repeat the process with the three remaining strips. Then run a line of glue along the length of one of the oval petals and place the wire on the glue. Fold the petal in half before opening it out again (fig. 233). Repeat this process with the four remaining petals. Bind these petals so that they are evenly spaced around the centre spikey ones and curve them inwards gently so that they enclose the somewhat complicated centre. Any material which will not fray would be suitable for this flower, in particular silk organdie and papers of various kinds.

## ROSE ON COWEE PICK

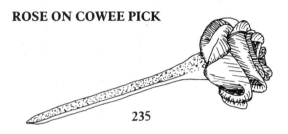

235

**Materials**

30 cm (1 ft) 1.2 cm (1 in.) wide ribbon
Cowee pick

This rose is made according to the instructions on page 63 but with the following variations. First, as the cowee pick forms the stem, join the ribbon to the top of the stick with the attached wire. Then make the entire rose without using the wire to secure the folds. At the completion of the rose, bind the end of the ribbon with the wire. Cover the base of the flower and the stick with tape.

**GOLD-AND-WHITE TABLE DOME** 236

This table dome is in gold and white. The gold in the dried ladies mantle was not really intense enough, so twenty-four roses on cowee picks were added. These were made from gold-coloured grosgrain ribbon which gave an interesting texture without the shine of some ribbon.

# MINIATURE SILK ROSE AND BUD

237

238

239

240

**Materials**
Thai or Indian silk
1 bead 1 cm (⅛ in.) in diameter
Spray paint

Cut four discs according to the pattern (fig. 237) with four rose-shaped petals on each one. Spray the centre of each disc very lightly with paint. Curl the edges of all the petals outwards. Thread the bead onto a rose wire. Twist the ends together and bind this to the top of a stem wire so that the bead touches the stem itself. Thread one of the layers of petals onto the stem and apply glue to the surface of the bead. Draw the petals up over the bead so that the first one encases the bead completely and the other three overlap to form the central bud. Repeat this process with the three remaining layers, placing the petals carefully so that they are irregularly spaced and secure each one with glue. Increase the number of layers according to the size you wish your rose to be. Remember for a larger rose, use a larger bead in the centre. For the sepals, cut four very narrow strips of green silk and glue these to radiate from the stem at the back of the rose or bud.

241

# WAX WATER LILY

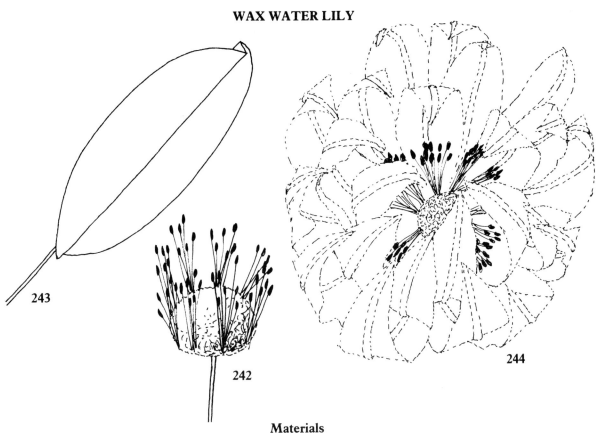

243

242

244

**Materials**
1 styrofoam ball 2.5 cm (1 in.) in diameter
1 bunch single-headed green stamens
White tarlatan
Milliners' wire
Melted wax

Separate the bunch of stamens into twelve equal parts and bind each group to a minute piece of stem wire, allowing them to protrude 2.5 cm (1 in.) above the wire. Insert these into the styrofoam ball so that they make a ring of stamens (fig. 242). Cut the tarlatan into twenty-six pointed oval petals 10 cm (4 in.) long according to the pattern (fig. 243). Apply a line of glue to the length of one and place a piece of milliners' wire onto the glue. Fold the petal in half before opening it out. Repeat this process with the remaining twenty-five petals and insert each one into the styrofoam ball starting just below the stamens, curving each one inwards. When all the petals are inserted they should radiate in approximately three layers around the centre. As water lilies traditionally rest on the top of water, no stem is required for this flower. Many substitute materials can be used. Once the flower is completed dip it into melted wax to make it waterproof.

# 3 Home

One advantage of making your own flowers is that they can be put in unlikely places where fresh flowers would not survive and they can also be made out of materials which have already been used in furnishings, so as to extend the colour scheme without adding too many additional colours. It can be argued that these materials might appear too heavy for flowers. That is possibly so, but if these are combined with dried grasses and some light silks, the contrast of the two materials will create the lightness required.

It is worth taking a look at your home with a view to making some flowers for it. Consider each room carefully and individually. The living room or sitting room will inevitably have more spaces which would take a spray of flowers or even a floral picture and may have a fireplace with a mantlepiece, window sills, a strip of wall between two doors and possibly an occasional table, and you may even like to put flowers on top of the television set.

The dining room, however, presents a different opportunity for floral decorations. The centre of the table is the obvious one, but there may be a sideboard, another fireplace, walls and the window too. If you have a piano, it is always preferable to put an arrangement of home-made flowers here, whether it is a grand piano or an upright, as there is no chance of any water spilling on this valuable instrument.

Your entrance hall may well have a table, chest or almost certainly a wall space between doors which would house a floral decoration.

The decorations in bedrooms should be light and continue the colour scheme. You may well have a dressing table mirror or space on the dressing table which would take the flowers, as indeed would a bedside table or cupboard door handle. Decorative window hangings look good in a bedroom.

The bathroom would take flowers either suspended from the ceiling or possibly on a glass shelf or in the window. Flowers here are always welcome as the furnishings are inevitably somewhat severe. Window decorations and hangings are suitable for most rooms, particularly in the living room where small floral sprays can be hung for example from keys in a book case, or from the structure supporting a lamp shade on a standard lamp and, of course, from the windows too.

245

## GOLD TABLE DECORATION

For the centre of a table a small compact low arrangement is always the most effective, not least because it allows an uninterrupted view across the table. This design is made entirely with paper. The gold gentians (*see page 53*) are made from gold foil crepe paper; some have gold outside and some inside, according to whether they are to be viewed from the side or the front. The little coaster flowers (*see page 54*) are brown and this colour is extended through the chenille bulrushes (*see page 24*) which lighten the design itself. A touch of sparkle is achieved by the addition of gold beads on little wire stems made into sprays of three. This design is arranged in a low vase in which the flowers are quite closely packed together, allowing the beads and the bulrushes to give a shimmering halo.

## IVY WITH HAY BALE

There are times when a small touch of flowers on a corner of a piece of furniture can have an interesting decorative impact. Situated here on a pine dresser the little hay bale is used to support the flowers (fig. 246). The main ribbon chrysanthemum (*see page 35*) is surrounded by artificial grass paper leaves from which flow sprays of ivy made with ready-made leaves. There are also three wired leaf camelias (*see page 15*) included to extend the floral area.

## CARNATIONS

Where a very simple, narrow, floral arrangement is required this line of flowers is simple and effective. The three wood fibre carnations (*see page 22*) have two floral alliums (*see page 29*) behind them to continue and accentuate the vertical appearance. In fact the only flower which is not vertical is the lower carnation bent slightly over the rim of the vase. The colours for this arrangement are red, chosen to contrast with the white vase.

247

## PICTURE

One interesting form of floral decoration is a picture, into which various furnishing fabrics as, for instance those used in curtains, cushions and chair coverings, can be incorporated. As relatively heavy materials are used here it is advisable to choose as large a frame as possible. This one measures 76 x 86 cm (2 ft 6 in. x 2 ft 10 in.) into which is put a hardboard backing covered with dralon velvet. The flowers are all placed vertically as though they are growing in a garden. All the stems and spaces below the flowers are filled with feathers, cut to simulate grass. These are goose feathers which are trimmed and curled at the tips. The five big single taffeta roses (*see page 51*)

have satin centres with gold stamens around them and are placed irregularly with the eight double taffeta roses (*see page 51*) intermingled with them. The material used for the double roses is a very deep shot taffeta which is a mixture of peacock blue and black and the two daisy stems (*see page 51*) are made with the material frayed which shows up the brightness of the pale blue. The vibrant turquoise of the single roses is echoed in a paler version with the five feather lilies (*see page 55*) which have gold stamens in the centre. These small touches of gold are included to balance the gilt in the frame. The five stems of pussy willow (*see page 23*) are made with

**ORCHID FERN**

grey chenille as are the six chenille stars (*see page 24*) which again have gold centres and this colour picks up the second colour of the frame. Floral pictures can be revived if they begin to look jaded by holding the whole picture over steam for a few minutes.

It is interesting to add home-made flowers to a foliage plant and here the touch of silver created by sprays of silver bouillon orchids (*see page 34*) make a delicate combination with this fern.

**250**

## WALL PANEL

This is an arrangement (fig. 250) designed for a bedroom where pictures do not seem particularly suitable. The main area of the room has plain wallpaper but one part is in this wallpaper (fig. 250) which has branches woven within the paper itself. Furnishing materials from the curtains were used to make the fifteen rose buds (*see page 50*) and the main flowers (organdie roses [*see page 50*]) are made with callico sprayed with old-rose paint to match the pink satin which is used to cover cushions. The other colour in the backgrond is mushroom brown, so a matching satin has been used to make the leaves. All the flowers and leaves are made separately and attached to the paper with a glue gun; the bare branches are now adorned with flowers.

## FLOWERS FOR A FIREPLACE (see colour plate 2)

During the summer it makes a welcome change to fill the empty grate with flowers. Felt and dried plant material have been combined for the arrangement in colour plate 2. The colours have been carefully chosen to tone with the mahogany furniture in the room and the turquoise carpet. The eight felt begonnias (*see page 37*) are made in deep petrol blue. The seventeen felt arum lilies (*see page 36*) are a pale mushroom, whilst the five felt dahlias (*see page 43*) pick up the deeper brown. The woolly leaves (*see page 57*) are made with shaded chunky wool which pick up both the brown and the turquoise. There are various kinds of grasses, some of which are dyed turquoise to lighten the effect of these some what heavy flowers, and dried eucalyptus is used to give a silvery brown which blends well with the felt. Arranged in a dark wood Tuscany basket, the whole design is elevated by a kettle stand.

# 4 Gifts

The addition of floral decoration can turn the most simple package into a personalized gift. Since these flowers will inevitably be thrown away, choose the simplest of designs. Remember also that most gifts will be tied in some way so whatever kind of spray is used it should be combined with the tying material – ribbon, cord or tape. Sometimes a floral decoration can be used to give emphasis to a box rather than as a means of securing a parcel. Flowers can be gifts in themselves, whether large sprays and bouquets of fresh flowers or small hand-made posies or scented sprays. They can be made entirely of flowers or of flowers with lace, pot-pourri or even candies tied in decorative paper.

In Austria a traditional floral craft incorporating all manner of cullinery spices is popular. Seeds, pips, cones and seed cases are combined in various floral forms and, with the addition of the pot-pourri, the aroma lingers enticingly for months. The musky scent of cloves and annis stars is the longest lasting.

The appearance of these natural materials somewhat muted as they are all within the brown, cream, grey and black colour range. This can be lifted by the use of a gold or silver springing called bouillon which can be used compressed or expanded and, where necessary, inserted with supporting wires. Some or all of the natural material can be sprayed with metallic paint to match the bouillon. Where further additional colour is required, a few flowers can be added. The forget-me-not type is the one most frequently included but the choice of colour for them needs careful consideration. The natural material has a certain look of antiquity, so any flowers should enhance this rather than create too much of a harsh contrast. One or more shades of one colour more effective than multi-colours. Ribbon is often used, usually velvet or grosgrain which should be the same colour as the flowers. Posy frills and ribbons are a traditional accompaniment to spiced work; not the lacey frills but solid cotton ones to match the flowers should be used, or gold and silver ones to match the bouillon. Since the actual choice of spices depends entirely on what is available, the instructions which follow suggest one type of material, but many variations can be made.

## SCENTED SPRAY (see colour plate 4)

The little spray in colour plate 4 is designed as a present for Granny or as a welcome gift for someone in hospital as the gentle aroma from the pot-pourri will drift from the bedside. The little spray is a combination of seven scented organdie roses (*see page 50*) and seven scented organdie buds (*see page 50*). The old rose spray which has been used to tint the flowers is accentuated by the five satin buds (*see page 50*) interspersed between them. Finally, a bow of pale velvet ribbon combines happily with the colours of the flowers.

## POSIES

So many different materials can be used for posies. Size is of the utmost importance. The desired appearance is a cluster of tiny flower heads with ribbon, grasses or leaves.

The seven ribbon roses (*see page 63*) are interspersed with heart-shaped pearls and paper leaves (*see page 57*) made with cotton cut-edge ribbon.

The spiced posy which accompanies it, is an assembly of dried poppy seed-heads (*see page 90*), nuts, cones, cotton moulds rolled in spices clusters of forget-me-nots (*see page 28*) in velvet, and single ones made from calico with a clove in the centre. The metallic grosgrain ribbon picks up the gold bouillon of the poppy seed-heads and the subtlety of colour is lent by a gentle green spray of paint on the calico flowers which echoes the colour of the posy frill itself.

251

## COATED COTTON MOULDS

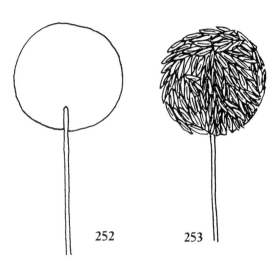

252    253

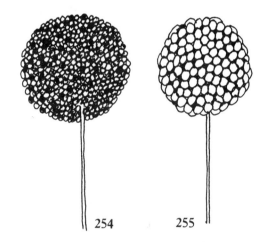

254    255

**Materials**
Cotton mould
Seeds
Glue

Glue a cotton mould to the top of a stem (fig. 252) and coat the entire surface with glue. If the mould is too absorbent it may be necessary to allow the first coat to dry and then coat it again. Dip the glued mould into the seeds and press extra ones onto it so that the entire surface is evenly coated.

Light seeds are the best to use, such as caraway seeds (fig. 253), poppy seeds (fig. 254) or black, red, white or mixed peppers (fig. 255).

## WIRED SEEDS

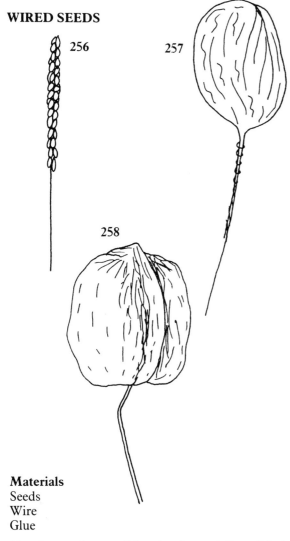

256

257

258

## SEED FLOWERS

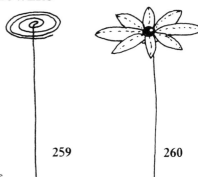

259

260

**Materials**
Seeds
Covered stem wire
Glue

Work the wire into a flat spiral leaving a straight end from the centre for the stem. Coat the surface of the spiral with glue and arrange long seeds to radiate around the central round one. Melon pips and sunflower seeds are suitable for the 'petals' and peppers or beans for the centres.

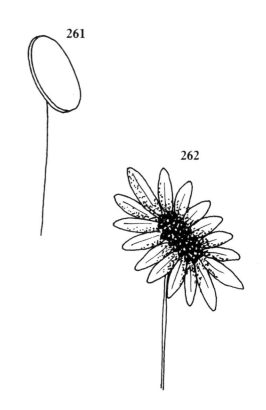

261

262

**Materials**
Seeds
Wire
Glue

Simply coat the top of the wire along a 2.5 cm (1 in.) length with glue and roll it in the seeds (fig. 256). Flowers made with bouillon (*see page 36*) can be incorporated as can nuts on stems (figs. 257 and 258), either sprayed or in their natural state. Nuts are hard to wire and the best way is to pierce them with a pin or pointed tool and insert a wire with glue into the resulting hole.

## LARGER SEED FLOWERS

**Materials**
Seeds
Card
Glue

Cut a disc 2.5 cm (1 in.) in diameter and glue a stem wire with a hooked top to the back of it (fig. 261). Coat the front surface with glue and arrange seeds as for the other seed flower (*see previous page*). The area to be covered in the centre is larger for this one so a pattern can be made with the central seeds forming concentric circles (fig. 262).

## FIR CONE FLOWER WITH PIPS

**Materials**
Fir cone
Melon pips

Insert a little glue between the scales of the fir cone and place the pips so that they radiate like a flower.

## CONE WITH BOUILLON

**Materials**
Cone
Bouillon

263

First wire the cone then stretch the bouillon springing and work a cobweb over and around the cone. By pressing the bouillon into the scales of the cone it will hold itself in position. The small, closely packed cones such as alder, larch or some South African species are best.

## SUGAR LUMP WITH BOUILLON

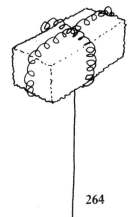

264

**Materials**
Sugar lump
Bouillon

Thread two rose wires each with 5 cm (2 in.) of bouillon and place them across each other on the top of the sugar lump. Twist all four wire ends together to form the stem and encase the sugar lamp like a parcel.

## ANNIS STAR WITH BOUILLON

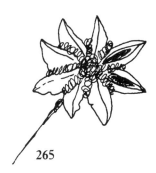

265

**Materials**
Annis star
Bouillon

Wire the annis star by threading 2.5 cm (1 in.) bouillon onto a rose wire and then looping this part over the centre of the star and twisting the wires together underneath to form a stem.

89

## POPPY SEED HEADS WITH BOUILLON

## WIRED CLOVES

266

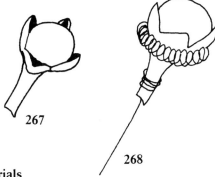

267

268

### Materials

First wire the poppy head then stretch the bouillon springing and work over the framework at the top of the seed head and press the bouillon together.

### Materials
Cloves
Bouillon

Choose nice big cloves with the central pip in place and wire this like a dried stem with rose wire. To attach bouillon (optional), first thread 2.5 cm (1 in.) onto a rose wire, keeping the springing condensed. Twist the ends together to form a stem and bend the resulting loop of bouillon at right angles to the stem. Insert the clove so that the star rests on the loop and bind the stems together.

## TRADITIONAL DESIGNS

Traditional designs can be made with these traditional materials, from miniature corsages with the materials tightly packed onto a leaf to large table arrangements, wall sprays, posies and hanging decorations to boxes with lids covered with cloves and seeds. All are time-consuming but fascinating to make. In small posies, larger arrangements and wall sprays, all the elements are held in position by means of twisting the stems to each other rather than binding with additional wires. No space should be visible between the materials, which should be flat. These compact designs are consequently extremely easy to keep and will last for years entirely justifying all the work that is put into them.

## BOUILLON BASKET

It is not always easy to show the scale of some of these designs, so this is why these flowers are sitting amongst coins (fig. 269), but it is not suggested that the money is part of the gift. A little tiny basket made with silver bouillon makes a charming present. The handle is made by threading two lengths of stem wires on to the bouillon and then twisting them together at intervals to create the loops between the twists. Join the ends together to form a ring. At the point where the ends are joined fix a cluster of five silk forget-me-nots and seven ready-made velvet leaves 3 cm (1¼ in.) long with seven bouillon leaves. This little design is very compact and is ideal if required to be sent by post.

269

## SPICED BOXES

Spice decorations give that special touch of luxury to a simple container in which there is a precious gift (fig. 270).

270

shaped confectionery leaves attached. Spotted 3 mm (⅛ in.) wide double satin ribbon hangs from this arrangement.

For Easter, decorated eggs look attractive hanging in the window. This one is made of styrofoam with 3 mm (⅛ in.) wide satin ribbon worked all over it and pinned into position. A cluster of miniature roses and buds (*see page 76*) decorate the top.

## HANGING DECORATIONS

If you are lucky enough to have large windows a hanging decoration in the German tradition can look pretty against them. They should be small so as not to absorb any possible light.

These three decorations (fig. 271) are made with tiny forget-me-nots (*see page 28*) and sprays of stamens, together with miniature artificial leaves. The bell and the basket also include cascades of 1.5 mm (¹⁄₁₆ in.) double-sided satin.

At Christmas it is nice to make hanging decorations to suit the season. The little ball (fig. 272) is a styrofoam shape covered with confectionery leaves and decorated with miniature roses and holly berries. Chenille is available in many metallic combinations. Here it has been made into a heart-shape with a cluster of holly berries and holly-

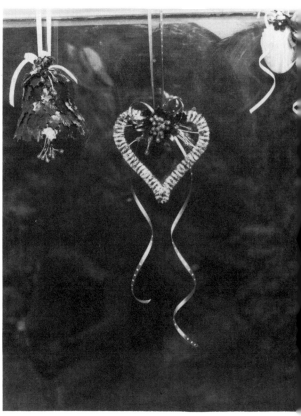

272

# 5 Weddings and Fashion

For many years flowers have been used for emphasis and as a feminine accessory to fashionable clothes. Quite often the material from garments themselves is used to make the flowers but remember that whenever flowers are to be worn, whether attached as corsages or stitched to dresses or hats, they must be extremely sturdy as inevitably they will not be treated too kindly, unlike those which are placed in a vase purely to be observed. Flowers in the hair should be light enough to stay in position without the help of a lot of pins.

A wedding is the traditional time to wear flowers – carnations for the men, corsages for the mother of the bride and groom, the bride's bouquet itself, the bridesmaids' flowers and also the headdresses. Since this is a very special occasion the bride will almost certainly have taken particular care to choose her wedding dress and so this attention to detail should be echoed in the flowers, either by matching the colours exactly or by using the same material, or by making identical floral bouquets and bridesmaids' flowers. Also the shape and style of these floral designs should echo those of the dresses. For example, if Victorian-style dresses are to be worn, then imitate the Victorian preference of floral sprays and posies with simple coronets for headdresses. For a modern style of wedding, however, dramatic flowers and suspended flowers on tubular covered stems, possibly using orchids, would be more suitable and the lines of the flowers should be clear-cut and simple. For the larger, frilly, billowing type of dresses, the flowers should be wistful, with sprays drifting in many directions, to enhance a dress rather than compete with it. Flowers for the bridesmaids should be in keeping with their age, for example, little baskets and flower balls are ideal for small children, but an older bridesmaid or 'Maid of Honour' would feel a little out of place carrying these rather childish designs and it is often preferable to make a miniature version of the bride's bouquet for these bridesmaids.

The style of the headdresses should be worked around the hairstyle of the bride and bridesmaids. The veil will most probably determine the hair style which the bride should wear, but for young bridesmaids it is advisable to make circlets or head-bands which are easily secured rather than several single flowers which may tend to slip out of their delicate, fine hair. However, when the bridesmaids are a little older, if they have long hair, this is the time to use individual flowers.

Hats are a perfect place for flowers, but how often does one see little bunches of miserable looking flowers? While being light to wear, they do not echo the more severe lines of the stiffer straw or felt hats. So, before making the flowers, examine the style of the hat you are to decorate and then make accordingly a string of flowers, a spray or one striking large flower.

273

## HAT

Little flowers can be put round the brim of a hat or a cluster or spray will nestle happily at the side of the crown, but for a dramatic effect use a large single rose like this one (fig. 273).

For this ribbon rose (*see page 63*) 2.74 m (3 yd) of 7 cm (3 in.) wide double satin ribbon has been used. The weight of the rose and the slippery texture of the ribbon make it difficult to handle and it may be necessary to make an extra bind of wire between each fold of ribbon to help retain its position. Two simple sprays of five leaves, one placed on either side of the rose give this flower a touch of reality.

## PARASOL

For a romantic wedding many brides prefer to have a parasol rather than the conventional bouquet. This one (fig. 274) is made of white lace over which cascade ready-made ivy stems and ready-made silk flowers. There is no reason to feel that the inclusion of a few ready-made materials will spoil the art of flowermaking when a deliberate contrast is required. The seven ribbon roses (*see page 63*) emphasize the colour of the silk flowers, while the three organdie anemones (*see page 49*) continue the colour of the white lace through the floral decoration. Pink single-faced satin ribbon 2.2 cm (⅞ in.) wide, is made into bows with long trails which are arrested in loops and swirls. Then, finally, one bow with very long trails is left to flow freely in the breeze, relying on gentle weather for the bride.

274

## 275   CORSAGES

For many years ladies have worn flowers, whether stitched to dresses, attached to pins in the form of a brooch or made into sprays and put through a button hole.

Figure 275 shows one or two ways of using miniature material. A bunch of two-tone stamens makes an interesting centre surrounded by ready-made silk leaves. Stamens can also be used to extend and lighten a compact floral area when miniature flowers are used as in these two little posies measuring 5 cm (2 in.) across. Miniature drawn-thread ribbon roses (*see page 63*) are used here and the numbers will depend on the size of your posy frill: approximately twelve flowers have been included in these posies. Little rings of flowers also make pretty decorative brooches. For this one eighteen little silk forget-me-nots are used, all of which have been taped onto one stem and the ends joined together to form the ring. The join is tied with narrow ribbon.

## BRIDESMAIDS' FLOWERS

For a little bridesmaid, this ring (fig. 276) is made of wired satin tubing plaited and shaped into a ring. Tiny forget-me-nots are threaded through holly leaf sprays and attached between suspended whirls of 1.5 mm (1/16 in.) double satin ribbon. All the materials are attached with glue so that the little bridesmaid can swing it all over the place with no fear of destroying the design.

For an adult bridesmaid or maid of honour, or for a Registry Office wedding, the elegant design in fig. 277 is made with six miniature silk roses (*see page 76*), five silk rose buds (*see page 76*) and twenty brown velvet forget-me-nots (*see page 28*). The colour of these forget-me-nots picks up the deep burgundy in the centre of the flowers which are two-tone, the second of which is light cream. This colour has been picked up in the velvet ribbon used to cover the three loops and is also used for the three velvet ribbon bulrushes (*see page 23*). Spray the silk roses to complete the design.

276

277

## MODERN BOUQUET

This sophisticated design (fig. 278) is made entirely with six tarlatan tiger lilies, the only additional material being thick chenille shaped into hearts, one for the flower and eight to accentuate the line in the centre. The ribbon is a sheer tri-stripe, black, grey and white, giving a striking appearance to this bouquet.

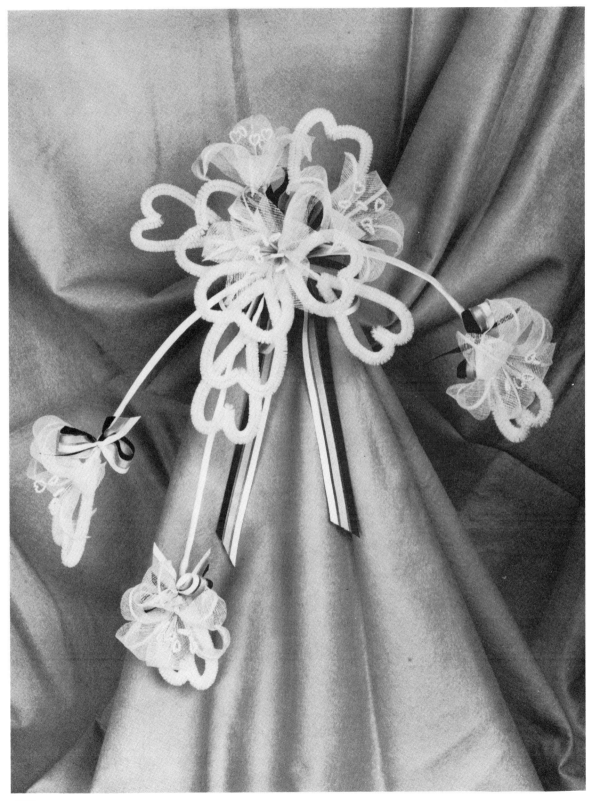

278

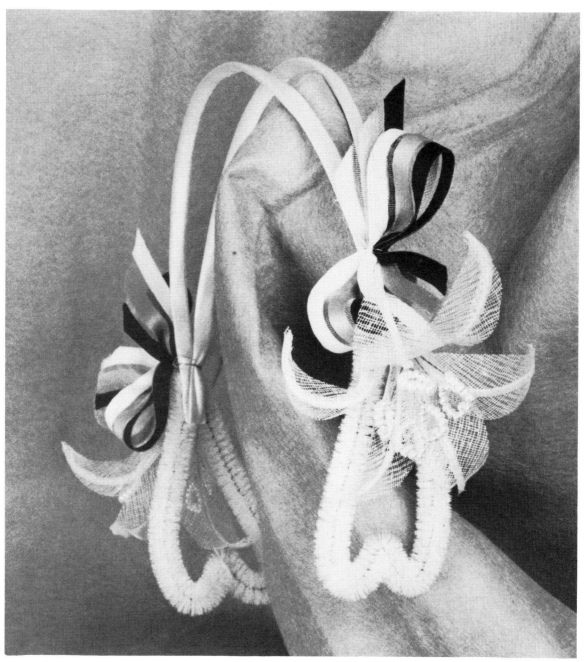

## HEADDRESSES

In figure 279 two arches of satin tubing inserted with wire are finished at each end with a small tarlatan tiger lily, one chenille heart and a bow of sheet tri-stripe ribbon.

This romantic circlet (fig. 280) consists of flowers made according to the forget-me-not instructions on page 28 with one crystallized stamen in the centre and two discs, one of organdie and one of tarlatan. Each little flower, of which there are sixteen, has a leaf attached to it. The bow of picot edged taffeta makes this headdress exactly match the romantic bouquet.

281

282

## BRIDE'S BOUQUET 1

This is a romantic spray for a frilly dress. The flowers in this bouquet (fig. 281) are made in accordance with the forget-me-not instructions (*see page 28*) using either a double layer of tarlatan, a single disc of lace, a triplicate layer of organdie, georgette and tarlatan, or a mixture of tarlatan and organdie. All the flowers have crystallized stamens in the centre. The little green rose leaves are ready made. The bouquet is put together with masses of picot-edged taffeta ribbon.

## BRIDE'S BOUQUET 2

This bouquet (figs. 282 and 283) is made entirely with ribbon roses, using a pale lavender iris colour, together with cream. Various widths of single face woven edge satin have been used to create this long cascade which would be suitable for a long lacey dress. The little cluster of flowers at the base of the

bouquet are those made for her headdress. The ivory satin leaves match the colour of the flowers and this creates a leafy outline. Matching satin ribbon has been used for the tie and the handle at the back of the bouquet. When the bride is standing, the tips of the ribbon reach right to the hem of her dress. To have a hand-made bouquet is something that the bride will cherish and keep forever.

283

**TUBING BASKET**

Bridesmaids love to carry little baskets of flowers. This design (fig. 284) is especially suitable for the little bridesmaid. A collection of wire leaf lilies (*see page 15*) is arranged with taped rose buds (*see page 69*) and sprays of matching, ready-made leaves. One flower is retained for the handle. The basket is made of satin tubing, as are the leaves (*see page 27*) and the handle is simply one long 37.5 cm (1 ft 3 in.) stem wire fixed underneath the flowers. Arrange the leaves so that during the wedding reception the basket can stand on the table as a floral decoration.

**FLOWER GIRL**

Sometimes flowers are all that is required to transform a plain outfit into fancy dress for a little girl. Only paper anemones (*see page 53*) are used here, both in the basket and for her coronet.

# 6 Special Places

This chapter is concerned with floral decorations which are made with a specific situation in mind. A summer fireplace, the corner of a room, an alcove, a specific window or the space between doors are places for which a floral arrangement can be designed.

## HANGING DECORATION

A lampshade frame covered with velvet ribbon is used for this hanging decoration (fig. 286). Wider ribbon is used to weave the base, into which is placed a styrofoam disc. Sixteen fuchsias (*see page 60*) hanging from the frame are interspersed with black chenille tendrills. The centre is filled with seven paper water lilies (*see page 60*) and the colour of the tendrils is echoed by those of the twisted paper leaves (*see page 57*). The delicate outline of the fuchsias gives an interesting pendulous profile to this arrangement.

286

## FELT DISCS

Where a narrow strip of wall needs decoration, such as in the bathroom or bedroom or beside the fireplace in the sitting room, this design would be ideal. It consists of three felt discs decorated with seven ribbon roses (*see page 63*) and twelve forget-me-nots (*see page 28*). The discs are joined by velvet tubing glued around the sides, with a knot tied between each one. To enhance the floral area, ready-made velvet leaves and little buds are attached with tendrils made by using the stems of the leaves and winding them round a pin. The addition of seeds completes the design.

## WAXED ORCHIDS

The striking, clear outline of waxed orchids (*see page 30*) combines well with paper leaves in this modern design enhanced by mirrors (fig. 288). Two sprays of waxed orchids create the height whilst three paper orchids (*see page 31*) are assembled at the base surrounded by paper leaves (*see page 57*).

288

## WINDOW GARDENS 289

Many flowers acquire a translucent quality when viewed with light passing through them. This spring arrangement (fig. 289) for a window is hanging from a ribbon-covered canework frame from the base of which spring sprays of forsythia, catkins and daffodils; a cluster of primroses nestles at its base.

## PURPLE TABLE DOME

A floral decoration to suit a low coffee table or the centre of a dining table can take the form of a dome (colour plate 5). Domes are very elegant and particularly suitable because they can be viewed from all sides. They are tightly packed floral balls, totally regular in shape. All the material here is worked on cowee picks and stuck into a foam base. The cowee picks give stability and are quick and efficient to work. There are times when the delicacy of dried flowers give the best colour combinations. Here the emphasis is on a very subtle shade of smokey grape combined with a buttery cream. It is best to work with the more robust dried plants first and then add the fragile ones; this minimises the risk of breaking any in the process. The cream colour has been picked up in the twelve miniature ribbon roses (*see page 63*) placed at intervals between the dried flowers. The catstail grasses are allowed to stand further out than the flowers to give the dome a shimmering outline.

### WAXED WATER LILIES

The use of wax makes these flowers (fig. 290) waterproof so they can float to no ill effect in water, with floating candles for a romantic evening.

### GOLD MIRROR

There are places where a large mass of flowers is required and yet too much hand-made material would appear heavy. Here (fig. 291) the arrangement of dried plants and grasses, all sprayed gold, was done first and then three paper zinneas (*see page 62*) and four paper peonies (*see page 61*) were accents of colour. Placed in front of a mirror the basic simple fan effect is multiplied into a luxurious arrangement.

291

## LILY DOME

This paper lily dome (fig. 292) was inspired by a ceramic design. Sixty paper arum lilies (*see page 36*) are laced into a styrofoam cone pointing upwards. Surrounding the rim of the vase is a circle of thirty paper leaves (*see page 57*) to complete this elegant paper centrepiece.

292

# **7** Special Occasions

Special occasions make the art of flowermaking particularly rewarding. Sprays can be assembled and suspended very simply when flowers are needed to be seen above the heads of guests at a party. To be effective from a distance, somewhat stylized line should be aimed for. Whatever the occasion, flowers can be made well in advance and stored in boxes, if necessary, for many weeks. If the flowers are very simple it is always more fun to get a group of people together to mass produce a large scheme.

## PAPER GARLAND

For a special festivity, bright colours are essential and in the scheme (in the colour plate on the back jacket) there is a definite Mexican accent. Use the pattern from the wax and paper water lilies (*see page 77*) but work one below the other to form a garland on a string. The four colours are used in rotation until the length of garland has been achieved. The disc in the centre is one wax water lily out of which falls a long paper plait with flowers on the end of each.

## MUSICAL EVENING

When stylized flowers are required for a stage or platform, tulips (*see page 58*) are ideal as their simple outline is easily recognizable. An additional advantage of choosing this type of flower is that, having only six petals, they are comparatively quick to make.

## TREE DECORATIONS

Ready-made tree decorations invite floral embellishment; here (fig. 294) each shape presents its own challenge. No specific instructions are given, as these are purely a few ideas. Sometimes the bells are attached to make simple big flowers and sometimes the flowers are made beforehand and then placed onto the shapes.

## ANEMONE TABLE

The theme of anemones made from crepe paper creates a scheme for this dinner party table (fig. 295).

293

112

## 296   GOLD RING

This arrangement (fig. 296) is worked on a vine ring, first sprayed with gold paint. All the materials are attached with a glue gun. Groups of poppy seed heads (*see page 90*) and rolled paper roses (*see page 54*) are entwined with gold ribbon before the whole design is encased in a cobweb of gold bouillon.

## DECORATIVE RINGS                                297

A little ring of flowers around a candle makes a very compact table decoration for an intimate dinner. It is, therefore, important to keep the floral area compact for safety reasons. In fact, it is possible to make decorative rings using only stamens. A solid ring of holly berries or green and white stamens with little green leaves around the edge is beautiful for Christmas. Velvet gives a luxurious contrast in texture to the wax of the candle and is used here in navy-blue for the forget-me-not ring.

## MODERN CHRISTMAS DESIGN

Three metallic lilies are grouped together at the base of this design, (fig. 299), out of which spring three metallic grasses of varying lengths. The whole spray is put together with extension wires which are then covered with black chenille to match the beads. This extension wire is shaped into a spiral to support the whole design.

### FAN         298

There are some beautiful fans available for decoration. This one (fig. 298) has been decorated to hang on the wall at Christmas. You could put it in place of a picture for the festive season. The material is first sprayed with two shades of colour with the deeper shade towards the centre and then attached to the fan with the glue gun. The five tinseltex chenille tendrils (*see page 70*) and fifteen leaves are ready made and some are partially sprayed silver. These form the outline into which three chenille flowers (*see page 25*) and a piece of artificial holly are displayed in the centre. Tiny pieces of cut chenille give the floral area a feathery outline with a cascading ribbon bow tied to the handle.

299

## CHRISTMAS FIREPLACE

It is possible to decorate a fireplace at Christmas, providing that care is taken so that the decoration cannot come into contact with the flames of the fire. There are many decorations to be made at Christmas and so there is seldom time for a lot of elaborate work. These sprays of holly leaves (*see page 70*) are simple, but effective. Cotton moulds are sprayed red to simulate holly berries and are worked into styrofoam balls with tartan ribbon. Tinseltex is used for the centre of the holly leaves and is allowed to hang down from the three vertical leaves.

# Appendices

## MATERIALS

So many materials can be used for flowermaking that, when this list was made, it was quite surprising to see the variation of possibilities. It is surely not complete; there must be many more which are worth considering.

### Basic materials
Floral tape
Stub/stem wires
Rose wires
Paper-covered wire
Milliners' wire
Binding wire
Cowee picks
Styrofoam
Floral foam
Plastic tubing

### Tools
Scissors
Wire cutters
UHU glue
Glue gun
Flower former

### Paints
Designers' watercolours
Spray paints
Crayons
Felt tip pens

### Ribbons
Cut-edge satin
Cut-edge cotton
Velvet
Velvet tubing
Satin tubing
Polypropolene
Woven edge satin and grosgrain
Picot-edged taffeta

### Dried materials
Dried plant materials – cones, seed heads
Spiced cullinery materials
Pot-pourri
Seeds and pips
Grasses
Nuts
Sugar

### Tissue
Foils and acetates
Flocked crepe
Single crepe
Double crepe
Jumbo crepe
Foil crepe
Artificial grass paper
Paper coasters
Plastics

### Fabrics
Butter muslin
Lace
Organdie
Silk
Felt
Calico/stiffened/dyed
Satin
Taffeta
Furnishing fabric

### Miscellaneous
Real leaves and ready-made leaves
Wax
Feathers
Chenille and tinseltex
Bump chenille
Bouillon
Stamens
Wool
Holly berries
Beads and sequins
Wreath frames
Baskets
Vases
Confectioners' leaves
Posy frills
Fans
Boxes
Glass hangers
Hay bales
Dolls' hair

## SUPPLIERS

*All supplies by mail order*
The Diddybox
The Nurseries,
Pinchbeck,
Spalding,
Lincs.

Flowerbrand,
87 Regent Street,
Kingswood, Bristol

**Floral foam, Wreath frames, Baskets, Silk leaves, Vases, Fans, Dried flowers**

Florists

**Ribbon**
*Offray Ribbon Ltd, Fir Tree Place, Church Road, Ashford, Middlesex

**Cut-edge ribbon**
Dryad Ltd,
P.O. Box 38, Northgates,
Leicester LE1 9BU

**Holly berries, Artificial leaves**
*Acorn, 129 Mildmay Road, London N1 4PT

**Wool**
Haberdashery

**Glass hangers**
**Miniature flowers and leaves**
*Dreipunkt Plastic H'Hofinger GMBH, Nordring, 35, 8156 Otterfing, W. Germany

**Posy frills**
*Walter Kunze, Papierverarbeitung, Max-Planck-Str. 6, Postfach 14, 8450 Amberg, W. Germany

**Miniature leaves, Stamens, Bouillon, Dried Materials**
*Ernst Rasp, A-5020 Salzburg, Gabelsbergerstrasse 19, Austria

**Cotton moulds**
**Beads and sequins**
Ells and Farrier, 5 Princess Street, Hanover Square, London W1

**Papers**
**Boxes**
Paperchase, 216 Tottenham Court Road, London W1

**Chenille**
**Styrofoam**
**Cowee picks**
Flowerbrand

**Fabrics**
Fabric shops

**Feathers**
**Dolls' hair**
Craftworkshop, St. Nicholas Market, Bristol

**Double crepe paper**
**Jumbo crepe**
Creative Crafts, 2 The Precinct, Winchester Road, Chandlers Ford, Hants.
*Cindus Corporation, 515 Station Avenue, Cincinnati, Ohio 45215, U.S.A.

**Wood fibre**
*Zimm's Inc., 4370 So. 300 West, Salt Lake City, Utah 84107, U.S.A.

**Hay bale**
The Diddybox

**Glue gun**
**Flower former**
*Steinel KG, Unit 9, Small Heath Trading Estate, Armoury Road, Birmingham B11 2RJ

**Felt**
*Bury Cooper & Whitehead, Hudcar Lane, Bury, Lancashire, BL 9 6HD.

*Note*
Those marked with an * are manufacturers. In these cases please write to Pamela Woods, Lyncombe Hall, Lyncombe Vale, Bath for your nearest stockist. As a lecturer, Pamela Woods gives classes in the art of flowermaking throughout the country. If you are interested, a calendar of venues is available.

# Index